W0114605

THE
BATTLE
FOR THE
BLACK
MIND

THE
BATTLE
FOR THE
BLACK
MIND

KARIDA L. BROWN

LEGACY
LIT

New York Boston

Copyright © 2025 by Karida L. Brown

Cover design by Dana Li
Cover art of "Remembering George" illustrated by Charly Palmer
Cover images by Shutterstock and Getty Images
Cover copyright © 2025 by Hachette Book Group, Inc.

Hachette Book Group supports the right to free expression and the value of copyright. The purpose of copyright is to encourage writers and artists to produce the creative works that enrich our culture.

The scanning, uploading, and distribution of this book without permission is a theft of the author's intellectual property. If you would like permission to use material from the book (other than for review purposes), please contact Permissions@hbgusa.com. Thank you for your support of the author's rights.

Legacy Lit, an imprint of Grand Central Publishing
Hachette Book Group
1290 Avenue of the Americas
New York, NY 10104
hachettebookgroup.com
Twitter.com/LegacyLitBooks
Instagram.com/LegacyLitBooks

First Edition: May 2025

Grand Central Publishing is a division of Hachette Book Group, Inc. The Legacy Lit and Grand Central Publishing names and logos are trademarks of Hachette Book Group, Inc.

The Hachette Speakers Bureau provides a wide range of authors for speaking events. To find out more, go to hachettespeakersbureau.com or email HachetteSpeakers@hbgusa.com.

The publisher is not responsible for websites (or their content) that are not owned by the publisher.

Print book interior design by Amnet ContentSource

Library of Congress Cataloging-in-Publication Data
Name: Brown, Karida, 1982– author.
Title: The battle for the black mind / Karida L. Brown.
Description: First edition. | New York, NY: Legacy Lit, [2025] | Includes
    bibliographical references.
Identifiers: LCCN 2024055719 | ISBN 9781538768433 (hardcover) | ISBN
    9781538768440 (paperback) | ISBN 9781538768457 (ebook)
Subjects: LCSH: African Americans—Education—History—19th century. |
    African Americans—Education—History—20th century. | Segregation in
    education—United States—History—19th century. | Segregation in
    education—United States—History—20th century. | African
    Americans—Social conditions—History—19th century. | African
    Americans—Social conditions—History—20th century. | Educational
    equalization—United States—History—19th century. | Educational
    equalization—United States—History—20th century. | United
    States—Race relations—History—19th century. | United States—Race
    relations—History—20th century.
Classification: LCC LC2741 .B76 2025 | DDC
    371.829/96073009034—dc23/eng/20250131
LC record available at https://lccn.loc.gov/2024055719

Printed in Canada

MRQ

Printing 1, 2025

To Charly,
You are my Love Supreme

If you are the big tree
We are the small axe
Sharpened to cut you down
Ready to cut you down
Sharpened to cut you down
Ready to cut you down

–Bob Marley, *Small Axe*

CONTENTS

Introduction

To Eat from the Tree of Knowledge

They say a mind is a terrible thing to waste. Well, as the chains of bondage fell from four million formerly enslaved people in the aftermath of the Civil War, the *Black* mind became a matter of national security

The South was in shambles, and even before the war, universal public education in the region did not exist for Black or white people. Schooling for the wealthy was private and exclusive, and for the poor, almost nonexistent. As the Southern school system began to take shape, around 1865, an argument festered that grew into a national fever. The question was, what kind of education should these newly freed Black Americans have—or should they have any at all? To most Black Americans, education was their North Star. Despite the seemingly insurmountable obstacles put in their way, they understood it was a key tool in guiding them on their journey toward liberation and self-determination.

The Battle for the Black Mind is the story of the epic struggle to seize control of Black education and mold generations of Black minds—a fight that began in the shadow of the Civil War and reached a boiling point with the landmark 1954 *Brown v. Board of Education* Supreme Court decision. It was a battle for the nation's moral conscience, one fought relentlessly in the classroom that still rages on today. Everyone was involved—Black and white, in America and in countries abroad. And the stakes were sky-high: the very future of Black education, and by extension, the soul of the nation, hung in the balance.

The struggle played out in classrooms but also in the highest courts of the land. *Brown v. Board* declared that America's "separate but equal" doctrine was no longer acceptable, taking a first step toward educational equity. Building on this momentum, Presidents John F. Kennedy and Lyndon Johnson issued several executive orders enacting affirmative action policies and civil rights bills aimed at repairing past harms inflicted on marginalized groups. However, decades later, in 1978, another education-related Supreme Court case—*Bakke v. Regents of California*—shifted affirmative action's focus away from directly addressing these harms enacted on specific groups toward the more amorphous concept of "diversity."[1] And most recently, in 2023, *Students for Fair Admissions v. Harvard and UNC Chapel Hill* rolled back much of the progress that had been made by barring race from being considered as one of many factors in college admissions. These cases set the tone for how America confronts, or often evades, its deepest issues about racial equity and justice that echo across generations.

And we all know that Supreme Court rulings do not exist in a vacuum—their spirits reverberate into every corner of society.

Today, the battle continues—and it's never felt more urgent. A war has been waged within the halls of our classrooms, communities, and poll booths across the country. With the second Trump presidency back in full swing and the promise of Project 2025 on the horizon, Black children, parents, and educators are entering a new era that threatens to dismantle decades of hard-fought gains in educational access and equity for our families. Books are being banned. Black authors are expected to stow away topics dealing with race, gender, or sexual orientation. Local school boards are fighting over whether they will allow the new AP African American Studies courses to be offered in high schools. "Stop Woke" laws are creeping into state legislation across the country, threatening to restrict educators from subjects considered "divisive"—which is really just a dog whistle for any topic that makes some white parents uncomfortable with their kids learning about our country's racist past and inequitable present.

Imagine a classroom where entire swaths of history are erased, where discussions of race are labeled "divisive," and where Black students are subtly, or at times explicitly, discouraged from seeing themselves as a part of the fabric in the rich tapestry of American life. This is not a hypothetical—under this administration, it is a promise. Under these new policies, many Black girls and boys will sit in classrooms stripped of books written by our greatest authors—luminaries like Toni Morrison and James Baldwin—without a chance for Black students to see their stories, their struggles, or their triumphs reflected. Lessons on slavery, civil rights, and the awesome contributions Black people have made to society could be whitewashed or silenced altogether. All to soothe the discomfort of a few. What these efforts show is that the classroom is where the core of American life takes shape. This was as true in the past as it is now.

This isn't just a matter of politics. It is an attempt to shape the worldview of an entire generation, to limit the horizons of Black children, and to make them strangers to their own history and culture in their classrooms. That's why *The Battle for the Black Mind* isn't just a history book; it's a road map. By looking back at the strategies and forms of resilience and resistance enacted by our ancestors, we can find the tools to not only survive what lies before us but thrive.

For Black Americans, education has always been a political act. During slavery, Black people went to incredible lengths to snatch bits of knowledge wherever they could—sometimes by hook, sometimes by crook. Despite laws that made teaching an enslaved person to read an illegal act, Black people found ways to learn. Fugitive sites of education—whether they were secret gatherings in cabins or in quiet moments amid grueling labor—became sanctuaries where Black minds could be filled with knowledge. Learning to read, write, do math, spell one's name, decipher coded language, and read maps were more than just functional skills. Each of these forms of learning was an act of defiance—a deliberate stand against a system that sought to dehumanize Black people by keeping us ignorant. Gaining these skills meant gaining some measure of independence, whether that was spiritual, mental, or physical.

Black people gained an education during slavery by any means necessary. Some slaveholders disobeyed the law and taught their enslaved to read, often because it made business sense. Most enslaved people worked in the fields; however, some labored in offices, printing presses, and other trades where literacy was a practical skill. There were also slave owners who believed it was wrong to deny Black people access to the Bible, making churches another avenue for education. Others learned by observing their white owners, eavesdropping on business dealings and teaching themselves, risking their lives and freedom for knowledge.

Then they would spin the block, bringing what they'd learned back to their communities, passing it on to their enslaved brothers and sisters. Tidbits of education passed along from their white play-mates. They learned math, reading, writing—fruit from the tree of knowledge that would nourish their Black minds and eventual destiny. But this was always done at a great risk. Those who dared to offer enlightenment to free or enslaved Black people put themselves in danger. Oppressors knew that knowledge was power, and educating Black minds threatened the very system on which they relied.[2]

As a NAACP award–winning author, sociologist, and professor, my expertise lies in two areas: studying how systemic racism works and exploring the rich history and culture of Black life. Over the past decade, I've had the privilege of teaching more than fifteen hundred undergraduate students on the history of race and education. My experiences at both a large, elite public university and a smaller, wealthy private university have given me the great opportunity to enlighten young minds not only about how racial inequality in education is perpetuated today but also to connect these present realities with the past. And that's the story I'm here to tell you in *The Battle for the Black Mind*.

In this book, I will take you through a century of separate and *un*equal education systems in the US, and how the epic battle for Black education became a global phenomenon, shaping Black schools in Africa, the Caribbean, and across the Black diaspora. This is a multiracial story, but at the center of it all, Black people have always played a pivotal role in building their own educational institutions. However, not all Black people think alike—we are as diverse a people as any in the world. It's a mistake, and frankly racist, to put us all in the same box. We will also explore the vast range of Black political thought around education that has brought us to the modern day, including by our heroes—some of whom may not be portrayed in the picture-perfect light in which you are used to seeing them. Others are unknown but need to be brought further into the spotlight.

Black people have always had their eyes on their freedom dreams. But the question of how to make them a reality has always been up for debate. And that debate is political.

The battle for the Black mind has been an ongoing war of ideas—a war over who and what Black people could be, a disagreement about our potential and state of being. Historically, many whites genuinely believed Black people were inherently inferior and therefore shouldn't have access to the same education as their children. Instead, they advocated for a curriculum that suited their perceived limited capabilities and present conditions of Black life.

How comfortable would you be with your children's curriculum—what they are allowed to learn in school—being determined by preconceived notions based on their race?

This was the stark reality of Black children for nearly a century following the Civil War. Dangerous ideas about Black inferiority found fertile ground in religious institutions, philanthropies, and local boards of education, creating a treacherous educational landscape that we're still trying to repair today. In response, Black educators fought hard to build independent Black private schools, often against a new and more subtle system of oppression that kept shape-shifting, but never stopped growing.

While I am more than capable of giving you a lecture on the history of Black education, what better way to tell the story than through the villains and heroes—people who were busy at work trying to build educational systems of oppression and those who fought to tear those systems down. In the end, this book reveals the love and passion, messiness, and absurdity of what it means to be human in a rapidly changing and often unjust world.

The battle for the Black mind has been an ongoing Cold War—a slow-burning struggle for control over the narrative, values, and future of Black education. The events in this book aren't isolated; they are part of deliberate, multidecade strategies, much like the promise of Project 2025. Plans like these begin as ideas, evolve into ideologies, and eventually drive political movements that crystallize into policy—oftentimes assaulting the core values that this country claims to uphold. So, too, was the battle for the Black mind. In the same way, the battle for the Black mind has been a relentless fight for autonomy, truth, and liberation set against the tides of the interests of the rich and powerful who are all too often dead set on maintaining control.

Martin Luther King Jr. is famous for saying that "the arc of the moral universe is long, but it bends toward justice." An arc isn't a straight line though, and it's certainly not without its pitfalls and setbacks. Our ancestors left us a legacy of educational excellence and a playbook for how to survive. We must understand this history, in all its complexity. Lest we take how far we've come for granted.

★ ★ ★

For over 150 years, historically Black colleges and universities (HBCUs) have been the engine of higher education for Black people in America. They continue to graduate more Black doctors, engineers, dentists, and professionals than any other type of higher education institution. But HBCUs are more than just schools—they are cultural heirlooms for Black people worldwide. They represent not just educational values but also sites of love, recognition, and celebration of Black culture and history. From historically Black sororities and fraternities—the Divine Nine—to archives that hold precious Black historical documents and art, HBCUs have been sanctuaries of Black intellectual and cultural life.

For decades, HBCUs were some of the only places where Black ideas could be presented, preserved, and celebrated. In the early twentieth century, Black artists who couldn't get their work exhibited in mainstream museums or galleries turned to HBCUs. These schools were more than just educational institutions; they were, and still are, places to gather. Much like the Black church in those days, they were the incubators of Black political thought, social movements, and Love.

But here's the part that may be uncomfortable: not all HBCUs were born out of Black freedom dreams. Many were founded on principles that had more to do with controlling Black minds than liberating them. I want you to know the origin stories of how our beloved HBCUs were founded, the principles upon which they were built, and how many of them evolved into the elite and powerful institutions they are today.

The reality is that most HBCUs were founded by white men—people with a range of ideas about what the Black mind was capable of. This doesn't mean that these schools are bad because of their origins, but it's important to understand their histories. It allows us to appreciate what we fought so valiantly for—to transform these institutions into spaces that are for us, by us.

But what does it truly mean to pursue liberation through knowledge in a system designed to suppress it? And how have the battles waged in classrooms and courtrooms across generations shaped our present-day fight for educational justice? How did we create a blueprint for resistance in a society bent on subjugating us? What lessons can we draw from our ancestors' resolve, and how do we apply them in today's struggle against new attempts to co-opt, censor, and undermine our learning? *The Battle for the Black Mind* not only lays out the strategies and tactics used in the past to attempt to control the Black mind but also highlights the countless ways Black communities have pushed back, reclaiming education as a space for freedom and self-determination.

As you journey through these pages, you'll find a playbook—a guide for navigating times when both the government and corporations aim to control what our children learn. You'll uncover actionable steps you can take to protect our educational freedoms, rooted in the wisdom and moves made by generations of Black people who have navigated even more troubled waters than the ones before us. We, as a people, have done this before. And we can do it again. This book is a reminder of the deep reservoir of resilience, wisdom, and self-determination that has always sustained us. And a call to dip into the well once more.

CHAPTER 1

Roots and Branches

As an educator, I know that a curriculum is much more than a mere list of subjects and assignments. It's a reflection of my educational philosophy—what kind of person, what kind of mind, I hope to cultivate in my learning environment. At its core, the curriculum addresses the fundamental question all educators face: What are the broader aims of education?

For many educators after the Civil War, that purpose was highly contested. The emergence of historically Black colleges and universities (HBCUs) tells this story.

Two of the oldest and most influential HBCUs in American history, Hampton University and Atlanta University, still stand strong today and have given us Black scientists, engineers, scholars, artists, journalists, and politicians—plenty of brilliant Black minds. But their origin stories tell us something deeper about the early struggle for Black liberation.

Hampton and Atlanta were founded within three years of each other, right after the Civil War, but they came to represent two very different visions for what a Black college could and should be.

Atlanta University saw education as the gateway to liberating Black minds, opening up new worlds of possibility, autonomy, and leadership. Hampton envisioned education as a way to keep Black people in their place, to train them as manual laborers. These two institutions became archetypes, each serving as a symbol of what Black education might achieve—or what it might deny.

Both schools were founded by the same organizations—the American Missionary Association (AMA) and the Freedmen's Bureau. The AMA established many of America's HBCUs, but the true vision came from their first leaders. School presidents set the course, and like true leaders, they created the mission—what should be taught, and how, and, ultimately, what the aims of Black education should be.

The clash began when they didn't agree on the answers. As a result, a war was waged over the curriculum itself.

Two warring ideas lived on opposing sides of the battle lines. Both would have a major impact on the landscape of Black education going forward. Atlanta University was rooted in liberal arts while Hampton embodied industrial education. These two philosophies—one that nurtured the mind and spirit, and the other that prepared Black people for manual labor—became the fault lines in a battle that would last for generations.

The first presidents of both Hampton and Atlanta were white men. But their views on Black education were worlds apart.

However, before we go on, there's a part of Hampton's story you must know.

The origin of Hampton University doesn't really begin with its first president, Samuel Chapman Armstrong. It begins with a Black woman named Mary Smith Peake. Born in the 1820s, forty-five years before Emancipation, this woman laid the foundation on which the university would be built. Her tears, sweat, and freedom dreams fertilized the soil on the land where the school would grow. The legacy of her audacious vision for Black education lives on today in its roots.

Mary's vision was Hampton's first seeds.

★ ★ ★

Mary moved through the town's byways like an undercover agent. Her students, too, moved in secrecy, stealing away in the dead of night to meet her. In a different world, their actions might seem ordinary. But here, in nineteenth-century Virginia, they were anything but. All of Mary's students were Black, and most of them enslaved.

In 1831, the enslaved Nat Turner led a rebellion that shook the very foundations of the South. Turner, a literate preacher, organized a band of fellow enslaved Virginians in a revolt that ended in the deaths of over fifty white plantation owners and overseers. Though Turner and his crew of freedom fighters were swiftly captured and executed, the fear they ignited spread like wildfire through the white South. Southern lawmakers reacted swiftly, passing harsh laws forbidding Black people—free or enslaved—from gathering for any kind of book learning. The classroom was outlawed, teachers were silenced, and the very thought of education for Black people was treated as a crime.[1] But Mary was undeterred.

Born in 1823 to a free Black woman and an absentee white father, Mary had circumvented Virginia's racist laws by receiving her education in the nation's capital, where free Blacks like herself could still legally access schooling. At sixteen, armed with a near-complete high school education, she returned to coastal Virginia to live with her mother and stepfather. By day, she worked as a dressmaker—a perfect cover for her true mission. By night, she worked in the shadows as a relentless liberator of Black minds.

An oracle of sorts, Mary's wide almond-shaped eyes saw beyond the oppressive reality around her. In her mind's eye, she could see a not-so-distant future where all Black people were free. Her clandestine lessons were time machines, transporting her students to a world where they, too, could see her freedom dream. She met them whenever and wherever they could slip into the shadows of privacy—slave cabins, wooded enclaves, anywhere away from the watchful eyes of white folks. Young and old, men and women, free and enslaved, Mary Smith Peake armed Black Virginians with freedom's ammunition: reading, writing, arithmetic, and critical thought. She unlocked the shackles of ignorance forced upon her people by giving them fruit from the forbidden tree of knowledge. In time, written letters transformed from symbols to sounds, and with quiet practice and diligence, words became worlds—untethered from the shackles of slavery. For her and her students, education was not just a path to freedom—it was freedom itself.

Southern whites understood this truth all too well. The power to control Black bodies depended on their ability to control Black minds. That's why they made it illegal for Black people to learn to read, write, or even to recognize their own names on paper. No one understood this more than the four million souls who were starved of an education. Supremely aware that knowledge is power, Black Americans have always gone to extraordinary lengths to seize it.

In 1847, Mary and her family left the city of Norfolk for Hampton, a coastal town where the air, tinged with salt and the muted grumblings of freedom, whispered of new possibilities. Here, she continued her covert classes. With hushed voices reciting their ABCs at the edge of the white man's plantation, her students continued to learn. For nearly twenty years, Mary smuggled books and knowledge through Virginia's plantations, at the risk of penalties ranging from fines of up to one hundred dollars (about $4,500 in today's dollars) to the risk of death.

Ironically, it was the chaos of the Civil War that finally brought Mary's underground operation into the light. In 1861, the Confederate Army burned the city of Hampton to the ground in an attempt to prevent the Union army from using it as a strategic base. Mary's family, along with many others, sought refuge at the nearby Union camp at Fort Monroe. There, formerly enslaved refugees were deemed "contraband of war," a title that protected them from recapture by their so-called owners. After two decades of defying Virginia's racist laws that tried to keep her people in the dark, Mary officially established her school in the light of day at Fort Monroe, teaching Black fugitives who had sought asylum with Lincoln's army.

On September 17, 1861, Mary gathered a dozen students, including her own five year old daughter, Daisey, under the shade of a majestic oak tree for their first day of school. Her class quadrupled in size within a week's time. Mary tirelessly delivered her lessons to Black minds who lay in wait at the precipice of freedom. As the country tore itself apart in a bloody Civil War, her students gorged themselves on the fruit of knowledge she provided under the shade of that oak tree.

Word of Mary's school soon reached the AMA, a New England faith-based abolitionist organization. It sent provisions to Fort Monroe, arranged a small salary for Mary, and purchased Brown Cottage, a modest home on the property where she could continue to teach. With its support, Mary Smith Peake became the first Black teacher of record of a Freedmen's Bureau School.[2]

Despite a persistent cough that worsened daily, Mary continued to teach. The fresh air brought in by the river wind didn't comfort her lungs much, but the simple beauty of the shaded lawn pleased her, nonetheless. When she could no longer walk to her oak tree, she taught from her bed in Brown Cottage as her students sat along the floor by her bedside, hanging on her every word.

In 1863, just one year after her death, the local community gathered under Mary's tree to hear President Abraham Lincoln's Emancipation Proclamation—the very first reading of the address to be delivered in the American South. Today, that tree—Emancipation Oak—stands as a national historic landmark on the campus of Hampton University.

Hampton University blossomed under that freedom tree.

Brown Cottage, Mary's home and schoolhouse, was the first building on campus. Its foundation was laid upon the fertile grounds of Mary Smith Peake's freedom dreams. Long before the school achieved global acclaim, it was a place where Black Americans stood at the crossroads of slavery and freedom, intent on freeing their minds from bondage.

Mary was an early and too-often-forgotten warrior in the long battle for the Black mind. Thousands of Black teachers, named and unnamed, risked fines up to $500 (approximately $20,000 in today's dollars), a year imprisonment, public flogging, and even slow death—all in order to wrench their own education from the grips of white supremacy and pass it on to others.

Over the years, the AMA remained committed to building institutions of education for the descendants of Emancipation, supporting Hampton and dozens of other Black schools across the South. After the war, it acquired two hundred acres of land west of Emancipation Oak, and by 1868, the Hampton Normal and Agricultural Institute was officially established. But Mary's vision for Black education—a vision rooted in liberation—would be a dream deferred. A new course in the battle for the Black mind was about to unfold.

★ ★ ★

As the dust settled from the Civil War, a wave of white missionaries from quiet towns of New England descended on the South, eager to build something new out of the ashes of the scorched earth. They came with a variety of motivations—some carried a religious calling, others felt a deep sense of patriotic duty—but they all believed they were harbingers of progress. They arrived in the New South as an army of well-intentioned do-gooders, convinced they could heal the wounds of a fractured nation.

The war was over and federal Union troops continued to occupy the South as a conquered ward of the state. This era of "Reconstruction," from 1865 to 1877, was intended to cast a wide federal safety net upon the South as the nation took the long road to recovery from a devastating war. The Freedmen's Bureau, a federal agency created to offer special assistance to America's four million newly freed Black citizens, sent thousands of these northern volunteers to lend their skills in service of rebuilding the nation. Many of them were educators, social workers, and clergy hailing from staunch abolitionist families. They saw themselves as part of a righteous mission to not only restore the South but also shape a new national identity—not northern or southern, free or enslaved, but American.

Two men who answered this call, General Samuel Chapman Armstrong and Edmund Asa Ware, were educators, and each would play a pivotal role in shaping the future of Black education. Their creations became blueprints for two branches of Black education, but the men's goals grew so far apart it's hard to believe today that they stemmed from the same tree. What started as two parallel missions eventually morphed into a battle over two competing ideologies of Black education.

For most of us, our first teachers are our parents. For Samuel Chapman Armstrong, his sense of mission as a teacher was practically ingrained in his DNA. His father, a Princeton-educated Presbyterian minister, didn't just answer a calling; he set sail on the *Aeverick* alongside his new wife, Clarissa, in 1832 to the Hawaiian Islands. Their mission was to convert the "savage" Indigenous Hawaiians into "civilized" Christians. The Armstrongs were part of the early wave of white settlers who arrived in the Kingdom of Hawaii, a full fifty years before the US government violently overthrew the Hawaiian monarchy and annexed the territory as the nation's fiftieth state. Samuel was born only a few years after his parents' arrival, in 1839, surrounded by a family whose tacit sense of superiority wasn't taught explicitly but was demonstrated through their everyday actions. They didn't just preach to the Indigenous people; they set up churches across islands, invested in sugar plantations, and, most notably, built schools. So impactful were his contributions to the early Hawaiian school system that Richard Armstrong, Samuel's father, would go on to be called "the father of American education in Hawaii."

However, it wasn't the sheer number of schools he built that left an indelible mark on the Kingdom of Hawaii. It was his curriculum. The fastest way to shape the hearts and minds of a generation is through the school system, and Richard Armstrong knew this. But his curriculum wasn't about teaching kids to read and write. It was designed to mold Indigenous Hawaiian children into what he believed "civilized" Christians should be. Richard Armstrong's curricula was based on three pillars: Christianity, citizenship, and manual labor. I want you to sit with that for a moment.

Imagine what it meant for an entire generation of children to be taught in school that their religion, their culture, their language, their very being wasn't enough—that in order to be something in this world, they needed to be remade in someone else's image. That's the kind of foundation Richard Armstrong's son, Samuel, would soon bring with him when he came to America to shape Black education in the post–Civil War South.

The growing presence of Chinese and American companies throughout the mid-1800s drove a great part of his mandate. The industrial sugarcane plantations were booming, and the boys' club of white planters, businessmen, and missionaries saw this economic surge as a chance not only to make life-changing profits for themselves but also to bring their "civilizing" mission to the Indigenous peoples of Hawaii. Richard Armstrong was no different. He saw an opportunity, a big one. His idea was to create a standardized education program, one that would serve the needs of this new industrial economy by molding Hawaiian children into plantation laborers—a workforce of people that would, in his view, pave their way to salvation through hard work.

At twenty-one, Samuel Chapman Armstrong, like an apprentice perfecting his master's craft, left the only home he had ever known to continue the family legacy in the United States. He earned a degree from Williams College, a liberal arts school located in his mother's birthplace of Massachusetts. Armed with a steadfast faith in his mission, he set out to "civilize" Black Americans through his educational program. Following in his father's footsteps, Samuel set out to save Black Americans by providing them with the "right kind" of education. His mission was clear, but Samuel's vision for Black education would soon collide with a radically different one.

Around the same time that Armstrong began designing his special blueprint for Black minds, another "white knight" was on the horizon, preparing to lay his own foundation for Black education in the South. Though they never met, their vastly different visions for Black education ignited an ideological battle that would have a stronghold on Black schooling decades into the next century.

★ ★ ★

Edmund Asa Ware entered the scene with the same kind of youthful ambition and bold certainty that had carried Armstrong across the Pacific Ocean. Ware enrolled at Yale University with a sense of invincibility typical of a twenty-something-year-old white male of his intellect and privilege. His family wealth and multigenerational New England roots removed him from the day-to-day worries of sustenance or status that may have plagued others without such born stature. While so many of his classmates joined the Union army, the bookish Edmund stayed his course and focused on his studies, shaping a passion for education that would carry him into his postwar career. He became a passionate teacher with an infectious fervor for liberal arts education. Post grad, he became a teacher at the Norwich Free Academy in Connecticut, a small school rooted in the New England abolitionist values. He took what he learned both as a student and as a teacher in the liberal New England school systems and brought these ideas as building blocks for the emergent Black education system in the South. His vision for Black futures couldn't have been more different from Armstrong's.

When the AMA offered Ware an appointment in Georgia, he leaped at the opportunity. First, he accepted an unpaid appointment as superintendent of schools in Atlanta, Georgia. Shortly thereafter, General O. O. Howard, cofounder of Howard University in

Washington, DC, and head of the Freedmen's Bureau, appointed him as Georgia's superintendent of schools for the newly freed Black population.

It was his job to lay the groundwork for a new era of education for Black Americans. Believing that freedmen deserved the same high-level education as their white counterparts, Ware built schools aimed at nurturing Black intellectualism and potential. In 1868, he founded Lewis High School in Macon—one of the first Black high schools in the state—under the auspices of the AMA and the Freedmen's Bureau. The school's curriculum was rich and included courses in literature, history, algebra, Latin, Greek, and geography as well as home economics and agriculture—all designed to elevate Black minds and feed their thirst for knowledge. Ware breathed life into the institution with his strong conviction that Black people possessed the same intellectual capacity as whites. He believed that schools should be open to all and that freedmen should have the opportunity to attain the highest level of educational advancement should they seek it.

Ware built Black schools in Georgia as though he had Lucy in mind—a Black woman who was a student in two of his schools and whose accomplishments we will explore later in the book.

Lucy Craft Laney entered Lewis High School the year it opened. Born free in Georgia in 1854, almost a decade before the Civil War broke out, Lucy's life was remarkable for her time. Her father had secured his freedom before her birth, negotiating his and his family's way out of bondage. Her mother continued to work for the family that once enslaved her, but now she worked for wages. Somewhere amid the color lines, the house mistress taught young Lucy to read, setting her on an educational journey that few Black people of her generation could even dream of.

While her mother toiled in the house during the day, Lucy devoured books in the family's library. Through literature, she spent her youth traveling the world and growing bigger than the confines of her circumstances. Her family scrimped and saved to pay her fees to attend Lewis High School. It was there where she was nourished with the building blocks of a liberal education that would lay the foundation of her life's work. Precocious by any measure, Lucy graduated Lewis High School at just fifteen years old. She walked out the doors of one of Edmund Asa Ware's schools and right into another one.

Long before the smell of cannon smoke consumed the Georgia air, James Tate and Grandison B. Daniels, two formerly enslaved men, founded the first Black school in Atlanta. It started in secret within the walls of Friendship Baptist Church, an all-Black church Tate and Daniels had cofounded in the 1840s. The church building was ravaged by the war, but in 1865, these two founders ensured their vision for Black education endured by transferring the school into the care of the AMA. The AMA purchased the school as well as the surrounding sixty acres of land. Tate and Daniels saw this transfer as a way to secure resources and longevity for the education of their people. The AMA expanded the school's reach in 1865, officially chartering it as Atlanta University—today known as Clark Atlanta University—the first HBCU in the American South.

While Atlanta University's origin story is rooted in Black self-determination—Tate and Daniel's freedom dreams—its first president was a white man, Edmund Asa Ware. This was not unusual. In fact, the vast majority of HBCUs across the country were led by white administrators and faculty, a reality that lasted well into the 1930s. Despite being Black institutions in name and mission, their leadership and resources were often dictated by white hands and dollars.

By the time Lucy arrived at Atlanta University in 1869, there was a small faculty of five women working alongside Ware getting the brick and mortar of the campus ready to welcome its first incoming class. Like many women of her era, Lucy was required to enroll in a college degree focused on teacher training. Educational institutions often steered women into teaching programs, as that profession was deemed socially acceptable for them. But she did not let that limit the scope of her vision.

Lucy attended the school wearing her parents' sacrifice like a crown of sun-kissed gold atop her head. She knew she belonged. However, it was not hubris that carried her. It was her love for learning and her desire to empower Black minds. She aspired to be an educational tour de force for her people.

Within a few years, Atlanta University was bursting at the seams with students—not just with coming-of-age high school graduates seeking a college degree but also with hundreds of formerly enslaved adult learners who attended literacy classes on campus. As far as Georgia's newly minted citizens were concerned, education was freedom. To them, even learning to sign their own name on a check and to read the headlines in the local newspaper was an act of radical self-liberation. The demand for classes was insatiable. Faculty members worked around the clock like they were running a twenty-four-hour manufacturing plant. Courses were offered in three shifts—morning, midday, and night. In its first year, Atlanta University enrolled fourteen hundred learners of different sorts—from part-time adult learners to full-time college students, like Lucy.

Ware remained resolute in his belief that he was doing God's work, guiding Atlanta University through its early years with a deep conviction that education had the power to elevate all people, regardless of race. On campus, faculty and students, white and Black, shared meals together at the campus cafeteria, where they would discuss topics of that day's reading and lightly debate their thoughts on pressing issues of the day. It was an environment that fostered intellectual curiosity, where ideas flourished freely, unencumbered by the racism that engulfed much of the South.

Atlanta University was a private school, established with an initial investment of $72,000 from the Freedmen's Bureau and the AMA. Ware began making his vision for a first-rate liberal arts institution a reality. In addition to its private endowment, the university also received a small contribution of $8,000 from the state treasury. By accepting local taxpayer dollars, Atlanta University came under the purview of the Georgia Board of Education. This state appropriation, accounting for roughly 10 percent of the university's annual funding, came with strings attached. Georgia state law required all educational institutions receiving any amount of government funds to be subject to an on-site review by an all-white committee appointed by the governor.

When the committee members arrived on campus, they were met with something that surprised them: excellence. At the time of the review, Atlanta University had 160 students enrolled in the college track. The committee's report described astonishment at the students' intellectual abilities and discipline. Members conceded that Atlanta University challenged the prevailing belief that Black people were intellectually inferior. They marveled at the students' ability to tackle complex mathematical equations, world literature, and foreign languages. Among these students who blew the committee members' minds was Lucy Craft Laney.

The report underscored the fallacy of the time, acknowledging, "There are many members of the African race who can attain a high grade of intellectual culture." Atlanta University's commitment to liberal education, it seemed, was undeniable. Humans were humans. The reviewers even went so far as to recommend the governor continue his support of the school, noting that "the funds placed in the hands of the managers have been wisely expended."

But even this glowing firsthand testimony from well-respected political appointees, including that of former governor J. E. Brown, was not enough to shift public opinion or political will. The following year, in 1872, the state of Georgia withdrew its support. Still, Atlanta University forged on. Fifteen of the students, Lucy among them, graduated from the college track—the university's first cohort of college-bred Black Americans.

Edmund Asa Ware remained president for twenty-eight years, during which time he cemented his educational values: rigor, self-determination, and equality. He died suddenly in 1895 while walking to work, collapsing just steps away from the home of Atlanta University faculty member and fellow Yale alumni Horace Bumstead. As though taking the baton on the second leg of an Olympic relay race, Bumstead assumed the role as Atlanta University's next president, carrying forward the belief in the transformative power of a liberal education.

Years later, W. E. B. Du Bois, one of the school's most celebrated faculty, praised the New England missionaries who flocked south, like Ware and Bumstead, writing that they brought with them "not alms, but a friend; not cash, but character." These educators weren't simply aiming to maintain the status quo—they sought to help uplift Black Americans by giving them the tools to move beyond the shadow of slavery's legacy. According to Du Bois, they came not with contempt and pity "but [with] love and sympathy, the pulse of hearts beating with red blood."[3]

But as Ware's vision for liberal education flourished, a different, far more constrained view of Black education was taking root elsewhere. Newly founded schools like Atlanta, Fisk, and Howard University stood in sharp contrast to other institutions that adopted curricula to keep Black people in their "place." This ideological difference was the crux of the battle for the Black mind, creating two divergent paths for Black education. As schools like Atlanta University continued their missions, another blueprint for Black education was being designed. Ware's dream of intellectual liberation would soon meet trenchant resistance from a powerful movement dead set on limiting Black minds to small quarters.

Samuel Armstrong trudged over one hundred miles through the blood-soaked soil of Cemetery Ridge. Boots tattered and body weak, he emerged as one of the living from the three-day Battle of Gettysburg—recorded as the deadliest encounter of the Civil War. With thousands of images of unnatural death and ungodly human suffering seared into his memory, he had long ago surrendered control over his fate. Nonetheless, he remained resolved that he had a calling that could not be ignored.

Upon arriving at Camp Stanton, he volunteered to dedicate the remainder of his army service leading African American troops. Although he considered himself more Hawaiian than American, he counted it an honor to fight alongside the people whose freedom would be the ultimate prize of a Union victory. Leading these men on the battlefield was one thing, but Armstrong's sense of duty transcended soldiering. He took it upon himself to establish a pop-up school at the base, where, between battles, he taught Black soldiers to read and write.

To Armstrong, the African American Union soldiers were similar to the Indigenous children of Hawaii whom his father once sought to "civilize." Like his father, Samuel Armstrong believed it was his duty to usher the minds of the oppressed and downtrodden into a new dawn of freedom. With valor and conviction, he continued his dual role as lieutenant and schoolteacher for the remainder of his time in service. By the end of the war, President Andrew Jackson nominated Armstrong to be appointed to the rank of general in recognition of his volunteer service in the 9th United States Colored Infantry and the 8th United States Colored Troops. Armstrong returned to civilian life and continued his mission by joining the Freedmen's Bureau, becoming an ambassador of Black education.

General Samuel Chapman Armstrong made his home along the lush green meadows that so gently hugged the curves of Virginia's Chesapeake Bay, just a few feet away from Mary Smith Peake's freedom tree.

In 1868, just one year after chartering Atlanta University, the AMA incorporated the Hampton Normal and Agricultural Institute. Samuel was appointed its first president. Originally created as a secondary "normal school," meaning an institution of secondary education aimed at teacher training, Hampton Institute aimed to produce the first generation of trained African American teachers and wage laborers. However, something was off.

Armstrong's vision for Black education focused heavily on preparing Black people for manual labor, farming, and domestic service—reinforcing the dangerous idea that the Negro's highest aspiration should be a life of contented subservience. The school's two-hundred-acre campus was a classroom. The students spent more time tilling, scrubbing, sewing, cooking, chopping, and farming than they did studying traditional academic subjects. Early Hampton graduates left with teacher's certificates in industrial education. Armstrong's vision for his graduates was clear: to serve as a training force in America's segregated elementary schools to teach Black children to accept their roles in society as manual laborers and domestic servants as a means to save Black children not only from external systems but from themselves.[4]

The school's dynamic of Black labor under white leadership was the foundation of Hampton's curricula and the core of Samuel Armstrong's invention—the "Hampton Idea," a curriculum that was deeply rooted in training students for a life of service, and reinforcing segregation and subservience. With an all-white faculty instructing an all-Black student body, Hampton's structure mirrored the racial power dynamics of the post–Civil War South.[5] Armstrong believed he was providing his students with the best education possible. The best for a Black person, that is.

Soon after Hampton's opening, a student would arrive who would become Armstrong's most famous disciple—a Black Moses who would carry the Hampton Idea to his people: Booker T. Washington.

Of the pantheon of twentieth-century Black leaders, Booker T. Washington was one of the few who had firsthand experience with the horrors of chattel slavery. For the early years of his life, his whole world was bound by the brutal confines of the plantation. With the overseer's watchful eye and worn cowhide whip never far from Black skin—of children and adults alike—Washington's young mind absorbed the cycle of never-ending toil and limited food rations. For him, slavery was not an abstraction.

Born on a Virginia plantation around 1856, Booker was a child of nine or ten years old when his family was emancipated. Once free, his mother, Jane, embraced her freedom by walking two hundred miles, children in tow, to join her husband in the Appalachian coalfields of Malden, West Virginia. There, as a child, Booker worked hard labor in the dank abyss of the town's coal and salt mines to help support the family. Life in the mining camp felt like his family had traded one form of bondage for another. The grueling labor and the wretched living conditions in the company-owned coal town did not at all feel like freedom to him.

One day while working in the mines, Washington overheard two men talking about a school that had opened nearby in Virginia where Black men and women were not only learning trades but also becoming teachers. Reflecting on this moment in his youth, Washington recalled in his memoir, *Up from Slavery*, "As they went on describing the school, it seemed to me that it must be the greatest place on earth, and not even Heaven presented more attractions for me at that time than did the Hampton Normal and Agricultural Institute in Virginia."[6] From that moment on, Hampton became the only dream he allowed himself to have.

After a year of saving, Washington willed his dream into fruition. He embarked on the four-hundred-mile cross-state journey in any way he could, traveling a few miles at a time by stagecoach and train. When he ran out of money, he walked. When he reached Richmond, Virginia, just seventy-five miles out, he had nothing left. So he picked up odd jobs for a few weeks to earn enough money to finally make it to Hampton. He arrived at campus broke and

THE BATTLE FOR THE BLACK MIND

dusty, unable to put up the few dollars to enroll. However, Washington convinced the head teacher to admit him by demonstrating he could add value to the institution. As a test of his will, she hinted that the recital room needed cleaning. Washington got on it without delay. He swept, dusted, and polished the room so thoroughly that she admitted him on the spot. He would defray his tuition by working as the school's janitor.

Washington graduated from Hampton in 1875. He taught as an elementary school teacher for two years and attended a year of seminary school before returning to the Hampton Institute to join its staff. He had become one of Hampton's star alumni—someone who not only embodied the institution's values but also carried them forward with devotion. Washington had fully embraced the Hampton Idea.

When Alabama state officials reached out to General Armstrong about a new secondary school for Blacks opening in the state, the Hampton president immediately thought of Washington for president. It was an opportunity to spread the Hampton model beyond his school's campus. More importantly, Armstrong recognized that a Black leader would be far more effective at convincing Black people to embrace the industrial education model than any white man could. Washington was the perfect candidate: his own life story as a slave turned educator, coupled with his unwavering loyalty to the Hampton philosophy, made him the ideal figure to carry the legacy forward. Armstrong knew that Washington would be simultaneously relatable and aspirational to the Black masses.

In 1881, Washington arrived at Tuskegee Institute to take on the role as the school's first president. He was just twenty-five years old, with only four years of education under his belt. Yet, General Armstrong trusted him implicitly to be a faithful lieutenant in the growing Hampton army. At the time, it was highly unusual for a Black person to lead an institution of higher education. As I mentioned, until the mid-1900s, most HBCUs maintained a white leadership structure, including universities such as Fisk, Howard, and Atlanta University. But Tuskegee wasn't just any school. It was an experiment in Black education designed to fulfill a white man's vision of what Black people's role in American society ought to be. Armstrong's strategy for Tuskegee: white leadership, Black management. One of Hampton's own, Booker T. Washington was the perfect figurehead. He could gain the trust of Black communities in a way that white educators never could while simultaneously maintaining the loyalty and confidence of the powerful white men who funded the institution behind the scenes (more on them later).

Washington's presidency at Tuskegee marked the continuation of Armstrong's legacy. He not only embraced the Hampton Idea but became its strongest advocate. For nearly forty years, right up to his sudden death, Booker T. Washington would wield immense influence over Black lives, solidifying the Hampton-Tuskegee model as a dominant force in Black education for decades to come.

CHAPTER 2

The Calvary

Educational choices for Black Americans rapidly expanded in the years immediately following Emancipation. By 1870, just five years after the Civil War, there were already twenty-two historically Black colleges and universities (HBCUs) established throughout the South, as well as in Ohio, Pennsylvania, and Missouri. Early institutions like Hampton, Fisk, Shaw, Morgan State, Atlanta, Morehouse, and Howard were all established during this transformative time. By 1880, the number of HBCUs had doubled—forty-five Black colleges and universities were up and running, serving as engines of Black excellence across the United States.

While a few Black students made their way into predominantly white institutions, such as Harvard, Vassar, Brown, Boston University, and Yale, those opportunities were rare and exclusively confined to the North. These individuals were "firsts" and "onlys" in every sense—often the only Black faces in their graduating class, opening doors for future generations of Black minds who would soon blaze trails at elite predominantly white institutions.

But the story of Black education wasn't just about the elite few who went to college. Across the South, thousands of small schools sprang up to serve Black communities, especially at the elementary level.

These schools were the product of self-determination, as Black people came together to build their own educational institutions. Pooling resources—from quarters and dimes to dollars—families and communities did whatever they could to make these schools a reality. If they didn't have money, they donated furniture, food, and whatever else they could scrape together to create makeshift classrooms. Small church schools, like that of James Tate and Grandison B. Daniels—the two formerly enslaved men who used the sanctuary of a Black church as their classroom to secretly found the first school for Black children in Atlanta—dotted the southern landscape, built by everyday Black people determined to educate their children.

The first thing African American communities did after Emancipation was build their own churches and schools—often housed in the same buildings. The African Methodist Episcopal Church (AME), for instance, which had broken away from the mainline Methodist denomination because of racial discrimination, was instrumental in this effort. By 1880, the AME had established two thousand Black schools across the country, most of them small and operating out of church buildings. These grassroots schools gave Black families the opportunity to send their children to school when public schools were either out of reach or simply didn't exist for Black children.

At the time, many communities, including those in major cities, didn't provide public schools for Black children at all. The public education system was still in its infancy, so in the meantime, Black communities did what they had always done: reached deep within their own reservoir of ingenuity and resources to create something out of nothing. These independent schools varied greatly in size, quality, and curriculum. Some were good, others not so good. Some were large, others small. The teachers weren't always formally trained, and many entered the classroom with limited education themselves.

To put it plainly, Black education in the 1880s was a hodge-podge. But we had to start somewhere.

Despite the unevenness, there was a major force helping to shape this educational landscape: the Freedmen's Bureau. During its brief existence, the Freedmen's Bureau established more than one thousand Black schools throughout the South—schools at all levels, from elementary schools to colleges and universities, including Hampton, Fisk, Atlanta, and Howard Universities. These schools were government-funded and represented a significant federal investment in Black education. In fact, the Freedmen's Bureau spent $5 million (around $130 million in today's dollars) to establish schools for Black children. This was a massive financial commitment, especially considering southern states were still dragging their feet when it came to funding public schools for either Black or white children. The bureau's efforts were a game changer because they laid the institutional infrastructure for the public school system as we know it today. While private schools played an important role, the key to ensuring access to education for all children was through a publicly funded system, and that's what the Freedmen's Bureau had begun creating. By the end of its first year, in 1866, the Freedmen's Bureau had enrolled nearly one hundred thousand Black children in public schools. These were not inferior schools—Black children were getting the same education as white children in northern cities, and it was a curriculum meant for all American kids, irrespective of race.

This was a vision of separate yet equal access, and it was happening at the federal, state, and local levels.

It's important to note that the Freedmen's Bureau was the US government's first social safety net program.[1] Long before the New Deal, Medicaid, Medicare, or the GI Bill, there was the Freedmen's Bureau. While later government programs were created to serve the country's most vulnerable populations—veterans, the elderly, and those impacted by the Great Depression—the Freedmen's Bureau's mission was to help Black Americans transition from slavery to freedom, from property to citizens.

And it was working. By the end of the Civil War, it's estimated that the Black illiteracy rate was around 90 percent. In just fifteen years, that rate had dropped to 70 percent—meaning 30 percent of African Americans had acquired literacy. That's tremendous progress, driven by an expanding network of schools that was still struggling to keep apace with demand. Despite all the advancements, there still weren't enough schools. In 1880, only about 30 percent of Black children ages five to twenty were in some form of school.[2]

At the same time, white children in the South had their own struggles when it came to accessing quality education. Take Georgia, for example. The state's school system was underfunded and disorganized. By the 1880s, there were no county-owned schoolhouses. Instead, schools operated in makeshift buildings, often donated for use without modification to accommodate students. Most of these schools were rural, and they ran on a short three-month term. Nonetheless, Georgia had more than twice as many schools for white students—4,517 compared to just 2,020 for Black students, underscoring the significant racial disparities in educational access. However, beginning in 1894, locally raised money allowed for nearly three thousand more rural schoolhouses to be constructed, an indication of growing public interest in expanding education.[3] While this was progress, the opportunities available to white children still far outpaced those for Black students, who were largely left behind as these new public schoolhouses began to crop up.

★ ★ ★

The 1870s was a decade of deep betrayal for Black Americans. Just as we were beginning to taste the fruits of citizenship, the rug was pulled out from under us in two significant ways. The first blow came in 1872, when the US Congress shut down the Freedmen's Bureau. At this point, the Freedmen's Bureau wasn't just responsible for setting up public schools for Black children—it was so much more than that. It had created offices to help reconnect Black families ripped apart by the brutalities of slavery, so they could find one another and reunify—oftentimes after decades of separation. Can you imagine the emotional power in that? To rebuild what had been systematically torn apart, before even thinking about securing jobs or homes, Black people first had to find their people.

The bureau also helped Black people navigate labor contracts with former plantation owners, ensuring fairer treatment and giving them a fighting chance to avoid situations that put them not too far from slavery. It even established the Freedman's Savings Bank, which gave Black Americans a place to save their money, earn interest, and apply for loans to buy land—something that had been out of reach for generations. When the bureau was dismantled in 1872, all this vital support vanished in the blink of an eye.[4]

It was a federal agency designed to repair the deep harms of two hundred years of racial slavery, and yet, after just seven short years—from 1865 to 1872—Congress decided it was time to move on. They felt there were more pressing matters to deal with than supporting Black Americans. Sound familiar?

We've seen this same pattern time and time again. Most recently with the energy that surged across the country in 2020 after the murder of George Floyd, where many companies, institutions, and even government agencies made bold promises to finally reckon with hundreds of years of racial injustice. Google, for example, pledged $50 million to support HBCUs. But how quickly did that momentum die out? How fast did companies tire of focusing on Black lives? Today, many of those same organizations have reversed course, with some—including Google and Walmart—leading efforts to dismantle diversity, equity, and inclusion initiatives both within their own walls and across national policy. In this same way, Black Americans witnessed the premature closure of the Freedmen's Bureau. Unfortunately, this was not the worst of it.

Just five years later came the Compromise of 1877, which completely dismantled Reconstruction. This was the result of a political deal that determined who would become the next president after a hotly contested election. Rutherford B. Hayes was given the presidency, but in exchange, his administration promised to bring Reconstruction to an end. The North was ready to wash its hands of its moral crusade for racial repair and let the southern states have their way, meaning that "states' rights" would prevail. But states' rights to do what? The answer became painfully clear. Almost immediately, southern states started passing what became known as Black Codes, which evolved into what we know today as Jim Crow laws. These laws stripped Black Americans of all the civil rights they had gained since Emancipation and plunged them right into a century of legal, lethal, racial oppression.

Reconstruction had been a time of progress for America— politically, financially, economically, and especially educationally.

But the Compromise of 1877 ushered Black people into an era of abandonment. To the white North, the compromise was a way to move on and position the country for the economic success from the incoming Industrial Revolution. To the white South, it was a victory for "states' rights" to determine their future.[5]

With federal troops withdrawn, southern states wasted no time enacting Black Codes. These stripped away every civil right gained after the Civil War. Black Americans lost the right to vote, were expelled from political offices, and were barred from living in white neighborhoods, dining at restaurants, or enjoying public parks. In every way possible, the fall of Reconstruction ushered in a new century of oppression for Black Americans. The betrayal wasn't just political; it was deeply personal. Imagine living through this time— the fear and uncertainty is unimaginable. Racial terror, lynching, and race riots swept the South. Black Americans faced the threat of white violence daily, and the federal government had washed its hands of the problem. As a result, Black schools were almost entirely placed in private hands for the next fifty years. Meanwhile, the American public school system—from elementary schools to high schools and colleges—was being built for white kids, with state and federal tax dollars, leaving Black kids behind.

Southern states were now free to start codifying racial segregation into law. Laws were put on the state books, making it punishable by fines and even jail time if Black and white children attended school together. These laws stayed in place for a long time, and their impact was devastating. All-white boards of education weren't at all concerned with fairly allocating resources. As a result, Black schools quickly became even more overcrowded, underfunded, and neglected. Meanwhile, white school boards were collecting tax dollars from everyone—Black, white, Asian, Native, and Mexican

Americans—but appropriating the lion's share of funds to legally segregated white schools. These laws had long-lasting effects that were later challenged in the courts, all the way to the US Supreme Court, and upheld. This is how the seeds of inequality were planted, seeds that eventually grew into a forest of racial exclusion—the system of separate and *un*equal that would govern American life for nearly a century.

And this history isn't so distant. In fact, my own parents went to school in this very system. My mother and father, who are alive today, attended "colored schools" in the southern towns where they grew up under Jim Crow. So, as we traverse this battle, I need you to see how these seeds matter to all of us today. They grew into big trees of inequality that have had long-term intergenerational effects that still haunt us. As a millennial, I'm the first in my family's generation to have had the legal right to attend any school of my choice and ability—something my parents were denied because of their Black skin. That right wasn't just taken away from them—it was systemically and institutionally withheld, robbing them of access to equal education and, with it, the full range of opportunities that education brings: jobs, networks, access to certain types of housing, and so on.

The freedmen's generation, those who experienced slavery and freedom, organized and agitated for public education, not just for themselves but for everyone. Their activism resulted in the establishment of public education for both Black and white children in the South. Before the Civil War, there was no public school system in the region for anyone. It was Black people—voting, demanding, and even starting their own schools—that pushed this forward. Black politicians elected during Reconstruction helped pass the laws that established state boards of education and allocated tax dollars for schools. This is how the American public school system in the South came to fruition—from the freedom dreams of Black people.[6] It is cruel how quickly the fruits of their labor were snatched from them to only feed others.

★ ★ ★

Even as Black families faced systematic exclusion, America was experiencing an economic revival. The Gilded Age was in full swing. The North was booming in the manufacturing, natural resource extraction, and railroad industries. As a result, a new class of ultrawealthy industrialists emerged.

These barons of industry saw an opportunity in Black education. To them, the population of newly freed Black Americans represented a cheap workforce just lying in wait to fuel their industrial machines. They came to the post-Reconstruction South with bags of money, offering to fund Black education. But this was not solely charity. It was an investment in maintaining a cycle of exploitation of Black bodies. For Black education, white philanthropy would prove to be both a gift and a gilded cage. As we will soon see, all money ain't good money.

Northern money flowed into the South, to make sure Black people stayed right where they were. And these funders did it with a plan, spreading their ideas like bees pollinating a field of flowers—at conferences, in churches, at schools, at the bank, and behind closed doors. This was the birth of what came to be known as "the Tuskegee Machine"—a network of powerful northern industrialists working behind the scenes toward the same goal of controlling Black education.

This marked a pivotal shift in the battle for the Black mind.

Initially, as I've mentioned, the fight was over whether African Americans should even have access to education at all. During and right after slavery, they fought tooth and nail to learn, in the face of great danger. And some white northern missionaries joined in to support that fight. But now, the stakes had changed. Support for Black education was no longer just about morality or giving Black folks a fair shot. Now it was about capitalism. Northern industrialists saw education as an investment in future laborers, and they expected major returns.

Right from the start, they latched onto General Armstrong's Hampton-Tuskegee model of industrial education. To them, Hampton and Tuskegee were perfect models for what Black schools should look like. As we learned in the previous chapter, industrial education was basically a more hands-off method of subjugation—a strategy taken from slavery's playbook. It promoted the idea that Black people needed an education adapted to "their place" in society.

In the 1880s, 90 percent of Black Americans lived in the South, mostly in rural areas. Most men worked as sharecroppers, field hands, or manual laborers. Black women filled roles as domestic workers, cooking, cleaning, and raising white children—often at the expense of attending to the needs of their own. To make matters worse, the convict leasing system preyed on Black people unable to find steady work. Under Jim Crow laws, Black people were arrested for "loitering," thrown in jail, and leased out to labor in coal mines and on farms through a loophole in the Thirteenth Amendment that allowed enslavement as a punishment for a crime. In many ways, the economy of the New South looked a lot like the economy of slavery, just with a new name.[7]

This historical context reveals the hidden link connecting industrialization and Black education. The Hampton-Tuskegee model of industrial education reinforced the idea that domestic work, farming, mining, and other forms of backbreaking labor were "Black Jobs." It ensured that education for Black people would train them for roles in a subservient labor class—a permanent underclass designed to support the industrial machine.

But here's the truth: The Hampton-Tuskegee model was more than just a curriculum—it was a full-blown ideology. Like Trumpism today or Reaganomics of the 1980s, the Tuskegee Machine ideology came with a meticulously crafted action plan. It was created *for* Black people but not *by* us. Equal citizenship? Full participation in American life? For most white Americans, these outcomes were never part of the thinking. The goal was to keep benefiting from Black labor without having to grant Black people true access to full citizenship or equal rights.

At this point, most American descendants of Emancipation had been in this country for five, six, seven, or more generations. To exclude them from full citizenship was cruel and outrageous. But that's the reality Black Americans faced in the post-Reconstruction era. And that is why this phase of the battle for the Black mind was shaped by the heavy hand of white philanthropy, with big-monied families like the Rockefellers stepping in to exert their influence over Black education. As we'll see, the history of white philanthropy in Black education is about more than just money. It's about who controls the narrative, who decides what kind of education Black children receive, and, ultimately, who gets to shape the future of Black America.

These philanthropies came to the South with a meticulous playbook for how they wanted to shape the education system for generations. They didn't go about it in an openly racist or confrontational way. Their approach was far more strategic. They had a quiet plan to capture the entire Black education system—one that they hoped nobody would notice until it was too late. Let's get into the story of how they began to make their moves, because once you see the strategy, you will understand the game.

★ ★ ★

After the Civil War, two major foundations—the Peabody Education Fund and the John F. Slater Fund—emerged as the first big philanthropies in the United States, setting the stage for how private wealth would influence education, particularly in the post-Reconstruction South. These new philanthropies were reflections of the sweeping changes brought about by the concomitant fall of Reconstruction and the rise of industrial capitalism. This era saw the North's growing wealth, built on the back of rapid industrialization, begin to influence Southern society, especially in education.

The Peabody Education Fund was established in 1867 by George Peabody, a wealthy banker from Massachusetts. With a massive $2.1 million endowment—a staggering amount for its time—it aimed to promote the "intellectual, moral, and industrial education in the most destitute portion of the southern states." But there was a catch: the fund only supported existing public schools, which, during that time, disqualified 99 percent of Black schools.

John Fox Slater, another wealthy industrialist, also saw himself as a philanthropist with a higher calling. Slater was born in Rhode Island and had built a fortune through his textile business. In 1882, just two years before his death, he established the John F. Slater Fund with a $1 million endowment. Unlike Peabody, Slater's fund specifically aimed to support the education of Black Americans in the South. On the surface, it was a well-intentioned and much-needed effort. But again, there was a catch: Slater Fund dollars would only support schools that adhered to the Hampton-Tuskegee model of industrial education.

To add insult to injury, the board of trustees overseeing the fund consisted of some of the most powerful white men in America. Dubiously, Rutherford B. Hayes—the former US president who brokered the compromise that effectively ended Reconstruction and left Black people in the firing line of Jim Crow—was appointed chair of the Slater Fund's board of trustees. Why would Hayes, after divesting from Reconstruction, suddenly become invested in Black education? It was suspicious to say the least.

Hayes was not alone in this endeavor. His fellow board members included former Supreme Court justice Morrison Waite, former Confederate soldier turned politician J. L. M. Curry, and several wealthy white industrialists. These were men who saw Black education as another mechanism for maintaining control of the American economy, not empowering a people. Both the Peabody and Slater Funds were led by influential, powerful boards of trustees tasked with ensuring that the foundations' missions were carried out. But, of course, their own ambitions and egos often took center stage.

Unlike religious donations that came from organizations like the American Missionary Association (AMA), these secular foundations were driven by the vision of a single wealthy individual. And the government was on board with it. In 1894, Congress passed the Wilson-Gorman Tariff Act, giving tax-exempt status to charitable organizations. This made it easier for philanthropies to grow and solidify their influence on public policy. Just like they do today.

Case in point, the Bill & Melinda Gates Foundation. Since its founding in 1994, this philanthropy has poured billions of dollars into public health initiatives around the world, especially in the fight against malaria and the push for vaccines. While the foundation's money has undeniably saved lives, there have also been unintended consequences. With its immense concentration of wealth, the foundation has shaped global health priorities, often drawing funding and attention toward issues it deems critical and away from other pressing needs that remain neglected. Often, it is the issues most important to the people on the ground that get pushed to the side. This kind of outsized control by philanthropists is not new. It mirrors the role the Slater Fund played in shaping Black education in the nineteenth century—offering resources but simultaneously narrowing the possibilities of what education could mean for Black children.

The Slater Fund was the first private philanthropic gatekeeper, shaping the direction of Black education with a specific agenda in mind. While the board members set the overall strategy, they were not the ones executing it on the ground. That responsibility fell to the "philanthropic agent"—an individual who traveled through the South ensuring that the schools followed the industrial curriculum. These agents acted as enforcers, making sure that the philanthropic vision aligned with the political and economic interests of the northern business elite. The story of the Slater Fund's first agent illustrates the double-edged sword of white philanthropy—offering much-needed investment in Black education in the post-Reconstruction South while simultaneously enforcing constraints that ensured its underdevelopment.

Slater's first philanthropic agent was a man named Atticus Greene Haygood. A Southern Methodist minister and president of Emory College, Haygood had the perfect credentials to bridge two worlds: the white southern elite and northern philanthropists.

In 1881, Haygood wrote a book called *Our Brother in Black: His Freedom and His Future*, which challenged white southerners to let go of their racial prejudices. In it he said, "The colored schools should have the support, countenance, endorsement, and cooperation of Southern white people. Reasonable and good people must feel kindly toward schools for negroes; if they do not, they are ignorant." While Haygood's message didn't sit well with many white southerners, it resonated with some liberal-leaning folks up North, including wealthy businessmen like John F. Slater.

In fact, Haygood's book was one of the reasons Slater decided to focus his philanthropy on supporting Black education in the South.

In 1882, when the Slater trustees offered him the job as the fund's first philanthropic agent, Haygood happily accepted. But he had one condition: he would keep his position as president of Emory College. His role as the agent was to be the face of the New York–based organization in the South. The trustees had the money and the decision-making power, but they didn't have Haygood's deep southern connections. His job was to visit Black and white communities, give speeches about the philanthropy's goals, check out the state of Black schools, and recommend which ones should get funding. And of course, the trustees expected constant updates—daily letters, formal reports, the whole nine yards. They wanted Haygood to figure out how to keep everyone happy while carrying out their grand plans.

But strategy was not in Haygood's skill set or character.

He was a man who believed in the power of human connections and making decisions based on the needs of the moment. He was an optimist, always seeing the good in people and situations. But the trustees wanted numbers, reports, paperwork. As time went on, the difference in their approaches created tension. Haygood started to feel more and more disillusioned as the gap between his vision and the trustees' demands grew wider. Still, despite this growing discord, there was no denying that the Slater Fund was making a difference under his leadership.

As soon as they stepped on the scene, the philanthropy began expending small grants to Black schools, providing much-needed financial resources to support teacher salaries, school supplies, and building maintenance. This was a vital intervention given southern states' refusal to allocate sufficient funds to support Black schools. However, they were careful not to step on Jim Crow's toes—only supporting Black schools that agreed to adhere to the limited Hampton-Tuskegee curriculum. Slater's name quickly became synonymous with progress, symbolizing a bridge toward national unity between the North and South.

Just a year into his role, the trustees approached Haygood with a proposition: leave Emory College and dedicate all his time to the Slater Fund. The idea of leaving Emory was heartbreaking for Haygood. Like many southern institutions at the time, the college was struggling financially as a result of the war. In 1883, Emory's books showed a measly operational surplus of just $93.55 after paying all the faculty. Haygood had spent much of his presidency just trying to keep the school afloat. So, with a heavy heart, Haygood struck a deal with the Slater trustees. He agreed to their request, but he made sure Emory would benefit from his decision.

In an 1884 letter to Emory's board, Haygood wrote, "I beg at this time, to present my resignation as President of Emory College, to take effect at the close of this term." But Haygood didn't stop there. He added, "I am very grateful to God that I am at this time able to announce to the Board that through the generosity of a northern gentleman connected with the work of the John F. Slater Board I am able to make full provision for the speedy payment of every debt of Emory College."This $25,000 bailout was a lifeline. It didn't just save the college from bankruptcy; it laid the groundwork for Emory's future success.

Atticus Haygood's story isn't just about saving Emory College—it's a window into a vicious cycle that defines the ongoing, systemic underdevelopment of Black education. Today, with an endowment of over $12 billion, Emory University stands among the nation's most elite and wealthiest American universities. Without that crucial bailout, the college might have succumbed to financial ruin and been lost to history. But what's often overlooked is that the wealth that saved historically white institutions like Emory often came at the expense of Black schools and Black futures.

This is personal for me. In 2021, I joined the faculty as a Professor of Sociology at Emory University, which is located just a stone's throw away from several HBCUs that still lack the resources they deserve. This ocean-wide disparity did not emerge by accident—it was set in motion over a century ago by men like Haygood, who used northern money to keep white schools like Emory afloat while sowing the seeds of inequality in Black ones.

And this story is bigger than Emory. It's part of a broader pattern of systemic exploitation that includes slavery. Many of the wealthiest and most elite universities in the US were built, quite literally, on the backs of enslaved Black people. Take my alma mater, Brown University, for instance. In 2003, Brown became the first major university to investigate its ties to slavery. What it uncovered was staggering: Rhode Islanders had mounted more than one thousand slaving voyages before 1807, and Brown University's wealth was inextricably tied to the transatlantic slave trade.[8] In response, Brown initiated a series of actions to begin reckoning with its past, sparking a wave of similar inquiries across the nation's top colleges and universities, including into schools like Harvard, Princeton, William & Mary, and, yes, Emory.

In 2019, Lawrence Bacow, then president of Harvard University, commissioned an investigation into the university's ties to slavery. It did not take the committee of campus faculty long to uncover that Harvard's legacy and success is inextricably linked to its deep participation in the transatlantic slave trade and chattel slavery. The investigative committee published its findings, stating, "We believe that Harvard's intellectual, reputational, and financial resources should be marshaled in its efforts to remedy the harms of the University's ties to slavery, just as past representatives of Harvard deployed these same resources and caused harm." In response, former president Bacow announced that Harvard is making a $100 million commitment to redress its ties to slavery. Whether they will make good on this promise remains to be seen.

On the college and university scene today, history is converging on us at every turn. It is a knee-jerk reaction to assert that issues like slavery, colonialism, and racism are things of the past that have no place in our educational systems, especially college campuses. These reckonings show that what happened in the past—whether it was the underdevelopment of Black education or the exploitation of Black labor—still shapes the educational landscape today.

All the while, Black colleges and universities have been systematically underfunded for decades, both by the government and by private donors. It's important to see this in the context of today's underfunding of HBCUs. Many of these schools are still woefully underresourced, with much smaller endowments compared to their predominantly white counterparts. In 2021, the federal government made promises to support Black colleges, but the road to fulfilling them remains long and unpaved. According to a recent report from the White House, public HBCUs have been historically underfunded compared to predominantly white institutions, especially those that are land-grant universities. Between 1987 and 2020, the funding gaps between HBCUs and non-HBCUs ranged from $172 million to $2.1 billion per state. These discrepancies have had a severe impact on student outcomes, making it harder for HBCU students to graduate without debt and limiting their educational opportunities. Even though some high-profile donations have been made to HBCUs in recent years, the endowment gap has only grown. On average, the endowment for public HBCUs is about 50 percent of what it is for predominately white institutions.

This chronic underfunding forces HBCUs to rely heavily on tuition and fees, which puts a significant burden on their students, who are more likely to come from lower-income families. And when economic downturns hit, HBCUs are left scrambling to cover their costs, often having to raise tuition just to stay afloat. So when we talk about the historical and ongoing disparities between Black and white institutions, it is essential to understand that this is part of a long legacy of racial inequity and injustice. The resources that should have gone to support Black institutions were siphoned off to prop up white ones. And the effects of that theft are still with us today. To truly grasp how deeply this legacy of underdevelopment and racial inequity in Black education is rooted, we must look back at its earliest architects.

Not long after he fully committed to the Slater Fund, Atticus Haygood found himself in a tough spot. He was stuck between the demands of the board of trustees and the expectations of the people the foundation was supposed to serve. As a southern gentleman with deep ties to the community, Haygood believed that his lived experience and insider perspective were more valuable than any distant report analyzing Black education in the South. Unfortunately, some trustees didn't see it that way.

"The undertones of the January meeting were to me utterly unsatisfactory," Haygood confided in a letter to his ally, Slater board president Rutherford B. Hayes. These annual board meetings in New York City quickly became something Haygood dreaded. He felt deflated when he realized that some trustees were more interested in studying Black people than in helping them. He worried that the focus was shifting away from action and toward endless analysis, noting, "There seemed to be a notion that the chief end of the Slater Board was to study the Negro Question." In other words, Haygood sensed that the board was getting lost in theory, losing sight of its original mission to uplift Black communities through education.

"It is preposterous," he fumed to Hayes. "Prolonged investigations," in his view, were a waste of time. Despite finding a sympathetic ear in Hayes, Haygood's hands were tied. As the philanthropic agent, he was the face of the foundation but had no real power. Every expenditure, no matter how small, needed board approval. This bureaucratic red tape made him especially wary of Slater treasurer Morris K. Jessup, whom Haygood saw as a serious roadblock. Wary of Haygood's decision-making skills, Jessup nitpicked and second-guessed many of Haygood's funding recommendations.

But it wasn't just Haygood who was frustrated. Some trustees were unhappy with him too, especially with how he communicated. His updates were casual and sporadic, just brief field reports here and there. But the trustees wanted detailed reports packed with data and analysis. They wanted to feel in control of the fund's impact and expected Haygood to provide the kind of in-depth, quantified updates that would justify their investments. It was becoming clear: Haygood wasn't the right fit for what they wanted. They needed someone who could deliver extensive data on Black education and handle the formalities of official business. Haygood, on the other hand, was more of a lone ranger who trusted his instincts and preferred to make decisions on the fly. He wanted freedom and autonomy, while the trustees wanted rigid oversight and accountability.

Haygood was also catching heat from his fellow southerners. Part of his job involved giving speeches to promote the Slater Fund's mission, trying to win support from both Black and white communities for its mission to expand industrial education for Blacks in the South. Despite the fund's focus on industrial education, Haygood still often faced hostility from southern whites.

An op-ed in the *Banner-Watchman* of Athens, Georgia, titled "The Future of the Negro," captured the kind of hostility Haygood encountered regularly. The author argued that efforts to uplift Black Americans were pointless, claiming, "The inferior must give place to the superior." The writer dismissed the idea of Black self-determination and suggested that Black people should remain "the servant of the white man." He criticized the use of white taxpayer money for Black education. He mocked Haygood's efforts, writing, "You had might as well try to change the spots on a leopard as to educate the negro up to a higher standard than that designed by the Creator for them to occupy."

This kind of criticism wasn't uncommon. Another op-ed, titled "The Negro—His True Status," showed just how much disdain southern whites had for Haygood and his northern backers. The author questioned Haygood's authority to speak for Black people and insinuated that he had been co-opted by northern wealth. The piece concluded with a warning: "Any system of education that disorganizes the industrial status instituted by the whites of the South is dangerous."

Haygood wasn't used to this kind of harsh criticism. The once-revered minister found himself under fire from both his own organization and his community. Despite the resistance, he soldiered on for eight years before finally resigning in 1890. Throughout his tenure, Haygood remained at odds with the Slater trustees over how to distribute the funds. He believed in spreading the money across the growing number of Black schools, but the trustees wanted to focus their support on a few select institutions that taught the "right kind" of education. Caught between the conflicting interests of northern and southern whites, Haygood eventually left the South to take a position as bishop of the Methodist Episcopal Church in California.

The Slater Fund's early work, however, was not in vain. It directed funds to support a range of segregated Black schools, providing buildings and teacher support. But its real legacy lay in promoting the idea of industrial education as a path for Black Americans. The philanthropy, knowing that the white South would never accept anything close to social equality, pushed for an education that seemed like a compromise. Black Americans would get the education they wanted, but it would be an education that kept them in their place, one that wouldn't threaten the social order of the Jim Crow South.

However, these northern industrialists didn't get their way just by sending checks. It took advocacy and ideas. This is how social movements are created. One of its best vehicles to spread the word was through conferences. Back then, there was no social media, no email, and no internet. Conferences were one of the only ways that educationists—including religious missionaries, college presidents, philanthropists, businesspeople, and teachers—could come together to figure out how to move things forward. They'd debate, present papers, network, and share ideas from one mind to another. By the time everyone went back home, all had picked up new thoughts and strategies, cross-pollinating what they had learned. This idea sharing is what really started to dictate the trajectory of southern education. This was the work of what became known as "the Tuskegee Machine."

One of the most important conferences during this time was the Capon Springs Conference. It ran from 1898 to 1914 and brought together hundreds of people who were interested in the future of southern education, with a lot of focus on Black people. They debated what should be taught in Black schools, and businessmen were a major part of these conversations. Therefore, the conference agenda focused on building an educational system that served the American economy. They didn't care about whether Black folks were truly educated. They cared about making sure Black education reinforced what was good for business.

Most troublesome about the Capon Springs Conference was that Black people had little representation in the room. This conference was supposed to be about reuniting the North and the South, but it really was about reuniting *white* America. Black folks were in the background of the picture but not really in focus. They were the subject of the conversation but never the authors of the ideas.

With the Freedmen's Bureau gone and Reconstruction over, the need for schools and trained teachers was more urgent than ever. Black communities needed more. More schools, more teachers, more opportunities. And while the Tuskegee Machine focused on farming and domestic service, their limited scope wasn't enough. Black people needed a broader range of educational choices. Who was going to become the doctors, the nurses, the chemists, the architects, the engineers, the artists, and the writers? Industrial education alone wasn't going to cut it.

Up until that time, Hampton and Tuskegee were just two schools among many. They were providing a service, and an important one at that. To be clear—there's nothing inherently wrong with industrial education. We need folks who are going to take on manual and domestic labor as a profession. We need vocational schools, we need tech schools, and we need liberal arts schools. But the problem was, at this point, the diversity of school choices for Black Americans was narrowed to the point that it limited our dream horizons.

The only schools these philanthropies were interested in funding were those that replicated the Hampton-Tuskegee curriculum, and that's where it became harmful.

The Tuskegee Machine removed school choice from Black families and shoved a singular curriculum down their throats. Schools that offered different options weren't getting funded, and without that support, they struggled to survive. The cavalry was coming, but it came with a lot of strings attached. Black folks saw the issue for what it was and didn't just sit back and accept it. They had our own vision for what education should be. They weren't about to let anyone dictate their futures. They pushed back hard against the limited version of freedom that was being offered to them. While the Tuskegee Machine was busy creating its schemes, Black people forged ahead, building and dreaming up a future far more robust than the one others tried to impose.

Education meant everything to us, and we were willing to fight for the right to learn on our own terms. Even if that fight was against one another.

CHAPTER 3

Welcome to the Thunderdome

The iconic beef between Booker T. Washington and W. E. B. Du Bois was the original diss tape. Never before in American history had we seen notable Black leaders put their business out on the street and fight it out on a world stage for all to see. Before Kendrick and Drake, Jay-Z and Nas, Biggie and Tupac, there was Washington and Du Bois. But these epic battles are more than just personal conflicts; they are the soundtracks that have breathed life and language into the issues defining Black political thought and culture at a moment in time.

The 2024 Kendrick and Drake battle was so much more than two rappers who just didn't like each other. Their tracks expressed the different politics and ideologies that they represented. The beef hinged on questions about authenticity, self-reliance, character, and what it means to believe in and be "like us." What does it mean to draw from the deep well of Black culture, creativity, and genius versus appropriating those assets and wearing them as a mask for a market? In a white supremacist society, to what extent should Black people rely on the money and guidance of their oppressors to get free? This forum of knockdown, drag-out debate is something that is imprinted in the DNA of the culture, and it is exactly what led to the conflict between Du Bois and Washington.

Anyone who knows an ounce about Black history is familiar with giants Du Bois and Washington. They each played a major role in shaping Black education and politics, and their ideas are still studied in schools and universities around the world. But the relationship between these two Black titans and how they came to blows tells a hidden story about Black America.

The Du Bois–Washington beef proved pivotal to the battle for the Black mind and has lasting effects on Black politics today.

Washington was clear. He championed the Hampton-Tuskegee model of industrial education. At face value, there is a lot to like about the concept of industrial education: Is having a good work ethic important? Yes. Is blue-collar work important? Absolutely. Did Black Americans hold an advantage in our knowledge of agriculture due to centuries of forced labor through slavery? Yes.

Washington's ideology hinged on an ideal of Black capitalism. He believed that if we worked hard, saved our money, bought property, and built our homes brick by brick, we would create a pathway for Black people to build power in America. Eventually, if we were rich enough, we would earn the respect of white America, and at that point, they would have no choice but to look at us as equal and grant us equity. But Black intellectuals like Du Bois and others saw his argument was deeply flawed, and even dangerous.

Du Bois understood that it is impossible to wealth and class one's way out of white supremacy. What did Black wealth matter if landowning entrepreneurs were legally prohibited from disputing contracts they entered into with their white counterparts? If they couldn't vote in political elections and couldn't sit on a jury of their peers? But could be called "Boy" on the street in front of their children and treated with disrespect daily. What good is money if one is treated like an animal? Injustices, large and small, create a system of oppression that cannot be solved with capital alone.

Money undoubtedly matters, but Washington was trafficking more than that. He worked in service of a white ideology designed to keep Black Americans repressed. The industrial education model of Black education was cooked up in a lab at Hampton Institute by General Armstrong, and Booker T. Washington became its spokesperson.

In 1881, he was appointed president of Tuskegee Institute, where he benefited from extraordinary financial and social support from wealthy white northerners. As he grew in prominence, Du Bois and many other Black leaders began to express their unease, as they viewed Washington's program as deeply problematic.

Since education was the most surefire vehicle for social and economic mobility in America, Du Bois was willing to take down one of his own kind to ensure the well-being of his people.

Each man had his own view, and it split Black politics in two.

★ ★ ★

"Ignorant and inexperienced, it is not strange that in the first years of our new life we began at the top instead of at the bottom," Washington declared, as he readied the packed audience for the crescendo of his career-defining speech. Posing as a visionary who had the foresight to see through the fog of misguided priorities, Booker T. Washington wagged his finger with disapproval at his misguided people. He faulted them for what he saw as misplaced ambitions. He expressed his disappointment that in the zeal of Reconstruction, for Black folks, "a seat in Congress or the state legislature was more sought than real estate or Industrial skill; that the political convention or stump speaking had more attractions than starting a dairy farm or truck garden." The handful of Black attendees sat in tense anticipation among the sea of white audience members, waiting with bated breath as they tried to process confusion about what Washington's strange opening remarks implied.

Washington was correct: freedmen had wasted no time exercising their full rights as American citizens. In the dozen years that comprised the Reconstruction era, nearly two thousand African Americans served in political office, including sixteen elected members of Congress. However, Washington's wild claim that, in freedom, Black Americans had pursued performative political representation at the expense of real economic stability and skill building was simply untrue. After three hundred years of being classified as property, traded as commodities on the open global market and owned by white so-called masters, African Americans had managed to purchase nearly fifteen million acres of land within their first three decades of freedom.[1] Most of it in the South; all of it cultivated by Black farmers. Black schools were also sprouting up all over the southern landscape, mainly through the steadied efforts of the Freedmen's Bureau, northern religious organizations, and everyday Black people who saw education as the elevator that would afford their families the opportunity to ascend to the mountaintop of liberation.

For a dozen years, from the end of the Civil War in 1865 until 1877, Reconstruction presented America a glimpse at what true democracy could look like. African Americans were not only free but also were accounted for, supported, and enfranchised as they came into their new collective identity as citizens. They seized the moment with a fervor that left no political, economic, or civil right unclaimed. For the first time, Black Americans voted and politicked, deeded and decided, and devoured as much education as their minds could stomach. However, this epic chapter in America's history was short-lived. Reconstruction's promise of democracy had been mercilessly suffocated by the tightening grip of Jim Crow's noose.

Most of the audience members were white men of industry attending solely for their own business interests in the South. They, too, sat in hesitant intrigue, open to hearing what the assiduous leader had to say. The silence was profound, punctuated only by the whisper of high cotton swaying amid the sticky humid September air.

His address opened the Cotton States and International Exposition in Atlanta on that fall afternoon. Historic in its own right, Booker T. Washington's was the first public speech to be delivered by a Black person to a racially mixed audience in the South.[2] Immaculately dressed in his iconic three-piece suit, glossed caramel-colored skin, he paced the stage with conviction and oratorical restraint as he conveyed his carefully crafted message. Like many biracial Americans of his day, Washington was the product of an unnamed white man's force on his Black mother—an enslaved woman who possessed neither the rights nor the personhood to decline his advance. Washington's light gray eyes pierced the audience as he stood before them—the very embodiment of what he argued was the problem at hand. He was both Black and white, enslaved and free, loyal to the southern soil through and through, yet a willing almsman of northern wealth. He prophesized to his majority white audience that the only way his beloved South would rise from the ashes of the Civil War and the abandon of Reconstruction was through cooperation and compromise. Claiming that "the laws of changeless justice bind the oppressor to the oppressed," Washington asserted that the fate of Black and white southerners was inextricably linked—they would either sink or swim together.

He had been coached for this delicate speech by his mentors and sponsors from the Hampton Institute, men such as board trustee Robert Ogden who represented financial supporters in the northern class. Towing the rhetorical lines of the Tuskegee Machine, Washington was firm that Black people's rightful place was in the South. To him, the only way to prosper in their birthright was under the white man's purview. As though he could hear the far-off rumbling of the coming stampede of millions of southern Black migrants who would soon culminate into the African American Great Migration, he delivered a preemptive strike: "To those of my race who depend on bettering their condition in a foreign land or who underestimate the importance of cultivating friendly relations with the Southern white man, who is their next-door neighbor, I would say: 'Cast down your bucket where you are'—cast it down in making friends in every manly way of the people of all races by whom we are surrounded." What happened next was astounding.

Without skipping a beat, Washington turned his appeal to the whites in the audience. He nudged them to jog their memories about how patient and docile Black people had been in slavery, suggesting that that feeling had not changed in freedom. He reminded them that Black people had already proven their everlasting loyalty to white life. They had done so by wet-nursing their children, at times at the expense of their own; tilling their fields under the blazing sun; and caring for master on his sickbed—sometimes in more anguish for him than their own family.

He assured the white audience members that for the most part, Black folks understood their place in society and had no intention of making hasty demands for more than what white folks were willing to allow them. Assuring them that "the wisest among my race understand that the agitation of questions of social equality is the extremist's folly."

At a moment's notice Washington broke his stoic character and shouted with the conviction of a traveling preacher at a Pentecostal church revival: His people were "ready to lay down our lives, if need be, in defense of yours" and would align their interests with whites in every way. In a quick pivot to salve their psychic wounds, the masterful orator uttered the words that assuaged every white audience member's fears. His closing remarks made clear that in no way did Black people expect or desire social equality: "In all things that are purely social we can be as separate as the fingers, yet one as the hand in all things essential to mutual progress." Washington dropped the proverbial mic, while the Black attendees stood there, mouths open, dizzy from dread and utter dismay rushing through their bodies as they watched one of their own so eloquently sell them down the river.

You can just imagine how the Black people in the audience reacted, their eyes wide with disbelief as they witnessed the words coming out of his mouth. It wasn't just "cast down your buckets." In the words of Malcolm X, he was basically saying "Massa, *we* sick."[3] Washington was promising that Black people were going to continue playing a subservient role to white people. And by doing so Black people would agree to put our dignity, rights, and respect in white people's hands to dole out when they believed we were ready for it.

This speech was iconic because it really built a new sense of trust among white America. They rallied around Booker T. Washington, not only as a person but as an idea, a symbol, and an emblem of hope. His version of Blackness was acceptable to whites in both the North and South. He was an ideal Black American leader, and he was propped up by white philanthropy with the hope that he would lead his people to the promised land through these ideas of Black capitalism and subservience. Washington had become the official power broker between the white and Black worlds, and the mascot for the Tuskegee Machine. On that humid September day in Atlanta, Booker T. Washington shed his nascent skin and came into a new body as the most influential Black man in America since Frederick Douglass.

As you can imagine, that did not sit well with many Black people.

Du Bois was undoubtedly the most highly educated Black American in the world. By the time he left school in 1894, he'd graduated with bachelor's degrees from Fisk and Harvard, a PhD from Harvard, and completed a doctoral thesis in economics at the University of Berlin. To his surprise, despite his accolades, no white university would offer him a job. He imagined himself joining the ranks of one of the beacons of American intellectualism, such as Yale, University of Pennsylvania, or his alma mater, Harvard. Instead, he would have to choose from the growing list of Black colleges in the South.

W. E. B. Du Bois arrived in Atlanta in 1897. He had accepted a faculty position at Atlanta University, after a short stint at Wilberforce. He found the religious overtones of campus life there too stifling for his taste. However, he did manage to convince his student, Nina Gomer, to accept his hand in marriage and accompany him on the scholastic adventure that lay ahead. Prior to arriving in the Peach State, the Du Boises spent a year and a half in Philadelphia, where W. E. B. carried out the first empirical sociological study in the United States, *The Philadelphia Negro*.[4] He had secretly hoped that his short-term appointment as "assistant in sociology" at the University of Pennsylvania would translate into a full-time faculty position at the study's completion. But he quickly accepted the reality that the prestigious Ivy League university had no intention of making him its first Black faculty hire, a feat that would not happen for another fifty years. Instead, Du Bois headed down south to the bustling Georgia city, determined to liberate his people using the only weapons he had—his mind and his pen.

He arrived a man of twenty-nine years, overly dressed vis-à-vis his peers, seemingly aloof with an intensity that made everyone around him think twice before they dared speak. His signature handlebar mustache slightly curved up and out, and his penchant for donning tails and top hats for no particular reason made the young professor stand out. However, in every other way, he fit right in at Atlanta University.

One thing about Black people and the way we show up in society—especially among one another—is that everybody's invited to the cookout. But sometimes, that openness is to our own detriment. Even though the seeds of beef had already been planted between Booker T. Washington and W. E. B. Du Bois with that infamous 1895 speech, these two Black titans, men who fundamentally disagreed with each other, still found ways to come together. They wrote together, sat on panels, and engaged in public forums. They were the Black public intellectuals of their time.

It's like what we see today with folks like Cornel West, Michael Eric Dyson, Kimberlé Crenshaw, and Nikole Hannah-Jones. They don't all think the same way, and they might fundamentally disagree on certain topics, but at the core, they all want Black people to be free. That same spirit was alive in our Black luminaries back in the day.

Take 1899, for instance, when a book called *The Negro Problem* was published. It included essays from Washington and Du Bois, among others.[5] And while all the other essays covered a variety of topics related to Black life, Washington and Du Bois chose to zero in on one specific issue—Black education. This is where they really started putting their cards on the table, laying out their opposing arguments for the future of Black minds.

Washington, as expected, pushed for industrial education. He leaned on the same arguments he'd been using since the 1895 speech, suggesting that Black people already had a foothold in agriculture and domestic labor, thanks to slavery. "For nearly twenty years after the war, except in a few instances, the value of the industrial training given by the plantations was overlooked," Washington wrote. In his view, Black people were being taught literature, mathematics, and the sciences, with "little thought of what had been taking place during the preceding two hundred and fifty years, except, perhaps, as something to be escaped, to be got as far away from as possible." He urged his readers to stop looking down on that kind of work and to start capitalizing on it. In his mind, slavery had given us these skills—so why not make the best of it?

Du Bois had a different perspective. For him, it wasn't just about what degree one earned—it was about the *purpose* behind that degree. What's the endgame of education? He framed it as a question: Is a school meant "to make men into carpenters, or is it supposed to make carpenters into men?" Du Bois's concern was about character building, critical thinking, and shaping a broader worldview for Black people. He believed higher education should cultivate the whole person—imagination, principles, expansiveness—not just train Black minds to "do."

While Washington was focused on securing economic stability—through a limited range of professions that he believed wouldn't provoke whitelash—Du Bois envisioned cultivating a Black identity rooted in self-respect, intellectual growth, and leadership. Washington's approach was more pragmatic. His perspective was this: for better or worse, we are living within the all-encompassing system of white supremacy. We don't have the power here, so we've got to work within the system. Let's quietly build wealth, buy land, and gain strength—without drawing too much attention.

Both believed their ideas should be reflected in Black schools. However, what started as a disagreement about the best path for Black progress soon turned into a full-blown clash of the titans.

Booker T. Washington's status as the white-appointed leader of Black America kept growing, so did his influence. Powerful white leaders regularly consulted him before making decisions about employment opportunities or where to direct funding for Black institutions. His presence in the media also created the impression that most Black people supported his ideas. Biographers have since uncovered that Washington and his wealthy supporters went to great lengths to control the narrative, even paying off certain Black journalists to write favorable stories. For instance, when *The New York Age*, a Black-owned newspaper, faced financial trouble, Washington discreetly bailed out the editor in exchange for partial ownership of the paper.[6] Maneuvers like this allowed him to maintain an image of Black unity and support for the Hampton-Tuskegee model that was crucial to his brand.

At first, with so few Black leaders of Washington's prominence, most Black people were understandably hesitant to publicly criticize him. But as the brutal reality of Jim Crow dragged on into the next century, more and more Black folks started to feel like they couldn't afford to remain silent. The pushback against Washington's agenda was growing, and it signaled the beginning of a new era in Black political thought.

In 1901, William Monroe Trotter, a Black Boston native, launched a newspaper called *The Guardian*. As the editor in chief, Trotter made the paper's mission crystal clear in one of its early issues: "We 'do' for colored humanity what the world has conspired to deny us. We will not apologize, and we will not retreat—the Guardian makes itself responsible for our collective deliverance. None are free unless all are free."

The Guardian covered all aspects of Black life, with a special focus on exposing the injustices Black Americans faced and highlighting various freedom struggles across the country. Trotter, a Harvard graduate, was quickly labeled a radical because he rejected the liberal idea of gradualism—the notion that Black folks should wait patiently for their rights. He was an outspoken critic of Booker T. Washington, and he used his newspaper as a megaphone to alert Black people about the dangers of Washington's industrial education campaign. "The colored people see and understand you; they know that you have marked their very freedom for destruction, and yet, they endure you almost without murmur! O times, O evil days, upon which we have fallen!" he exclaimed in one editorial.[7]

Trotter's frequent attacks on Washington and his ideas resonated with a growing number of Black Americans who were fed up. But it was Du Bois's 1903 publication of *The Souls of Black Folk*—the original diss tape—that truly catalyzed the historic battle and created a seismic shift in the way Black people debated among one another.

And it wasn't just about Du Bois. This marked a new era in Black political thought—one where Black leaders and communities began to openly disagree and grapple with different visions for the Black futures. Nearly forty years back, right out of slavery, there had been little room for public debate or differentiation; survival and unity took precedence. But now, at the dawn of the twentieth century, the growing complexities of Black life in America meant that diverse perspectives were taking root, and so were conflicts about the best way forward.

★ ★ ★

Everything changed in 1903. It was the year Du Bois dropped *The Souls of Black Folk*, which became an international sensation. Even today, it's one of the most widely read books in American letters, repeatedly republished and highly cited.

The Souls of Black Folk is a masterpiece on the meaning and feeling of being Black in America, written at the turn of the century—a pivotal time in world history.[8] This book captivated readers not only because of its eloquence but because it spoke directly to the hearts of Black Americans grappling with their place in society. As a professor, I always smile when I ask my students in my Sociology of Race and Ethnicity class, "Who's heard of W. E. B. Du Bois?" and nearly every hand shoots up. And when I ask whether they've read any of *The Souls of Black Folk*, most of those hands stay raised. That's the power of this book—it's still resonating and growing with us today.

One of the most significant impacts of *The Souls of Black Folk* was how it escalated the tension between Du Bois and his soon-to-be arch rival. In a chapter titled "Of Mr. Booker T. Washington and Others," Du Bois brought the smoke. He publicly challenged Washington's entire educational and political program. He wasn't just calling out Washington; he was outing the entire Tuskegee Machine. Du Bois explained that theirs was a dangerous path that encouraged Black subservience and turned away from the fight for civil rights and true equality.

In *Souls*, Du Bois wasn't attacking Washington personally, but he was exposing the false consciousness that the Tuskegee Machine represented. By this time, many Black institutions had adopted the Hampton-Tuskegee model, not just because they believed in it but because the philanthropic dollars from the North came with those strings attached. If schools wanted funding, they had to follow the model, whether they agreed with it or not.

The Souls of Black Folk was published by a small, progressive white publisher in Chicago, and it got widespread attention. The book was reviewed in major outlets like the *New York Times*, and it became the topic of conversation in the literary and academic world as well as in regular poor and working-class Black communities. As a result, Washington couldn't ignore it, and Du Bois became a target of the Tuskegee Machine.

Let me walk you through what that chapter in *Souls* says.

"The time has come when one may speak in all sincerity and utter courtesy of the mistakes and shortcomings of Mr. Washington's career," he wrote.

Du Bois pointed out that industrial education had been around for decades, championed by free Black leaders and organizations like the American Missionary Association (AMA), but Washington was doing something different. He tied these ideas together, poured his endless energy into promoting them, and transformed what was once a side track into the only path for Black minds. Du Bois saw danger in this and called Washington's approach "seeds of disaster."

Initially, many Black Americans were angered by Washington's compromises, but, Du Bois observed, as northern businesses started investing in southern enterprises, white America—tired of dealing with the "race problem"—embraced Washington's message of "peaceful cooperation." Eventually, even Black Americans started to fall in line, accepting Washington's leadership without question, and the voices of dissent grew quieter.

Du Bois was unapologetic in his critique of Washington's leadership. He believed Washington had sold out Black political rights for an economic promise that never fully materialized. He insisted, "If reconciliation is to be marked by the industrial slavery and civic death of those same black men . . . then those black men . . . are called upon by every consideration of patriotism and loyalty to oppose such a course by all civilized methods." For Du Bois, Washington's program was more about propaganda than progress. He warned: "We have no right to sit silently by while the inevitable seeds are sown for a harvest of disaster to our children, black and white."

Although *The Souls of Black Folk* made waves internationally, reviews from the white media were mixed.[9] But for Black people reading the book, Du Bois's words hit different. It was like the release of a game-changing album. Like every time Kendrick drops a new track in the ongoing battle with Drake—it sparks conversations, breaks the internet, and has people dissecting every lyric. That's what *Souls* did for the culture back then. Black people were energized by the renewed discussion about their future and what they would accept or refuse, even from their own leaders. It sparked a larger conversation about Black political awareness. Du Bois had drawn the line in the sand. And the time had come to pick a side.

Things unraveled quickly after *The Souls of Black Folk* hit the shelves in April 1903. Only two months earlier, Washington had extended an invitation to Du Bois to collaborate on a behind-the-scenes project called the Committee of Twelve. Although this new literary sensation didn't halt their cordial collaboration, it did add more strain to their fragile relationship. As Washington became increasingly focused on Du Bois's movements, he began to suspect that the younger scholar was stirring up dissent among other Black leaders, figures like Howard University professor Kelly Miller, prolific journalist and activist Ida B. Wells, Harvard-trained historian Carter G. Woodson, and news editor William Monroe Trotter. The truth of the matter was that this new generation of Black leaders simply peeped what Washington was up to and drew their own conclusions about his mission.

Nonetheless, when anti-Washingtonian sentiment erupted into outright violence, Washington and his powerful backers wasted no time in blaming Du Bois.

In July of that year, tensions boiled over at the Colored Business League's annual meeting, held at the African Methodist Episcopal Zion church in Boston. This highly anticipated event drew over a thousand attendees from New England's Black middle class—entrepreneurs, lawyers, doctors, clergy, and scholars—men and women dressed in their finest, reflecting the growing success and refinement of the city's Black elite. Booker T. Washington was scheduled to deliver the closing keynote address. Before the emcee could even finish introducing him, disgruntled audience members began to voice their disapproval. According to a local Black newspaper, Washington's appearance was met with "hisses, catcalls, and cries to 'put him out!'"

The situation escalated when the event's host, a staunch Washington supporter, called in the Boston Police Department to manage the rowdy crowd. But the police arrived with clubs in hand, and what began as a peaceful protest turned into violent chaos. Members of Boston's Black elite stampeded in panic, and soon enough, the police were beating anyone within reach. Some attendees fought back, leading to the injury of several officers. The women joined in, and one officer was dangerously wounded in the groin with a hatpin.

Another officer, along with one of the protesters, was stabbed during the brawl. In the end, William Monroe Trotter and two others were arrested and charged with inciting a violent riot.[10]

Although Du Bois wasn't present at the event, Washington, ever the tactician, quickly spread rumors suggesting his rival had orchestrated the entire incident. Boston banker-turned-philanthropist George Foster Peabody contacted several members of Atlanta University's board to voice his concerns that Du Bois had conspired with Trotter. Though President Bumstead assured Peabody that Du Bois was not involved, the damage was done. Dependent on donations from wealthy northern backers, the university trustees feared the association with Trotter's actions would cost them their funding. They convened an emergency meeting to discuss whether Du Bois should be fired from his faculty position at Atlanta University.

Du Bois, ever composed under pressure, did not wait for others to decide his fate. He wrote directly to Peabody, laying out his stance in no uncertain terms. "I have steadfastly condemned Mr. Trotter's action from that day to this—a fact that he will testify to," Du Bois wrote, firmly distancing himself from the riot. At the same time, he made his thoughts about Washington clear: "As between him and Mr. Washington, I unhesitatingly believe Mr. Trotter to be far nearer the right in his contentions . . . in these days when every energy is being used to put black men back into slavery and when Mr. Washington is leading the way backward."[11]

Du Bois's frankness had the university trustees clutching their pearls. They felt his letter was too bold, too direct for someone whose livelihood relied on the goodwill of northern benefactors. The final vote on his dismissal came down to an even split. In the end, President Bumstead cast the deciding vote to keep him, calling Du Bois's letter "frank and manly."

Meanwhile, Washington continued to play the role of diplomat. He maintained polite communication with Du Bois as they both worked on organizing the Committee of Twelve—a body intended to bring together Black leaders with differing viewpoints to set a national Black agenda. Washington wrote to Du Bois two months before the scheduled convening, expressing his hope that they could "agree upon certain fundamental principles" and correct any misunderstandings. But as they worked together, it became clear to Du Bois that Washington's words did not match his actions. Washington quietly appointed a third executive committee member to vote with him, effectively outnumbering Du Bois two-to-one on every decision. He made sure that any proposal to address civil rights or political equality was shot down, leaving Du Bois powerless within the group he had helped create. By the end of the year, Du Bois resigned, skipping the inaugural conference altogether.

Reflecting on this last attempt at collaboration, he confided in a friend, "whatever I can do to promote harmony, I will do, but I will not put myself under the control and command of Mr. Washington."[12]

By 1903, W. E. B. Du Bois's influence had reached new heights. He had become an international symbol for Black radicalism. His name alone inspired conversations, stirred emotions, and shook up the political landscape. And as Du Bois's star ascended, a chorus of Black voices began to join in the public of dissent against Booker T. Washington.

★ ★ ★

While debates around Black education waged on among the Black middle class—those few African Americans with college degrees or professional careers, primarily based in the North—Black students in the South were feeling the weight of the Tuskegee Machine first-hand. The ideological battle between Du Bois and Washington was confirming for many Tuskegee students that something wasn't right about the education they were receiving.

Books like *The Souls of Black Folk*, news articles, and public commentaries from people like Ida B. Wells, Carter G. Woodson, Timothy Thomas Fortune, and other Black intellectuals, created space for crucial conversations about the impacts of the education system being offered to Black students and what it meant for Black futures. This discourse allowed Black people—the ones who had been intentionally excluded from conversations about the direction of their own education system—a pathway to insert themselves into the dialogue. The debate had become a hot topic in Black media and households, buzzing through communities as everyday Black people across the country began to grasp and weigh in on the conversation.

The Du Bois–Washington debates around education gave Black students the vocabulary to protest and express their dissatisfaction, which was no small feat. Lodging complaints and making demands to one of our own did not come naturally to a people not far from slavery and stripped of rights.

Imagine being a Black student in the early 1900s, sent off to college with your entire family's hopes and sacrifices riding on you. Oftentimes, a Black family would have to pool all its resources to send just one child to college, with siblings pitching in through their own labor to help cover the costs. What must it have felt like to arrive at Tuskegee, only to realize that what you were getting wasn't an education, but a glorified labor camp? How would you go back home and tell your family, who had put everything into your success, that the school wasn't what the family had hoped it would be? That burden of carrying your family's hopes, your community's pride, and, most times, the weight of "representing your race" made it hard to contest anything, even when things were wrong.

And this is where the Du Bois–Washington debate becomes significant. It didn't just open up intellectual discussions; it gave Black students and families the space to voice their demand for something better.

After the publication of *Souls*, Tuskegee students, too, began to express their disappointment in the education they were receiving at the institute. It was imperative that Washington and his trustees maintain the illusion that Tuskegee was a well-oiled machine. However, this was far from the truth. Given the school's rapid expansion and international prominence, Booker T. Washington spent more time away from campus, mainly in New York, Massachusetts, and Connecticut, delivering speeches and fundraising to support the Hampton-Tuskegee idea. While the school maintained a robust Black faculty, the quality of education at Tuskegee was secondary to maintaining its public image.

Most students voted with their feet, choosing to drop out of Tuskegee instead of remaining to complete their degrees. As a result, in the first decade of the 1900s, the school averaged a 10 percent graduation rate. While students maintained a general sense of deference for their school's president, they began to express their discontent with the curriculum. In an attempt to quell rising student frustrations, in 1904, Washington agreed to accept written criticism and suggestions from current Tuskegee students.

One young man submitted a seven-page letter expressing his concerns. After effusively expressing his "intense love" for the school, he lamented that "the school month has been reduced to twelve days as against sixteen days." This 25 percent reduction in course hours put immense pressure on students to complete their work.

Further, the near-exclusive focus on manual labor and military-esque disciplinary style left students feeling like Tuskegee was more of a plantation than an institution of higher education.

Faculty imposed strict rules on students. The school had a rule for everything, from time, to manners, to cleanliness and behavior. Infractions earned students "conditions"—negative marks that accumulated on their records. Expressing grievance with the imbalance between the faculty's focus on rules and punishment versus the quality of education, the same student wrote: "Under this circumstance, the large number of conditions and wide-spread dissatisfaction cannot be avoided. The student is helpless." Likely aware of Washington's image-conscious nature, the student cautioned that, left unaddressed, Tuskegee dropouts might stir up "public sentiment against the school."[13]

They wanted more than an education designed to prepare them for a life under Jim Crow. They wanted an education that would prepare them for freedom.

But what did this mean for the millions of Black children who didn't have the chance to even dream of higher education? For those living in the South, access to even a basic education beyond the fifth grade was rare. This was their reality.

My grandfather Thornton Davis grew up during this time in Boligee, Alabama, where his educational future was cut short due to his race and zip code. Grandpa was raised in a family of sharecroppers—orphaned from his own parents and adopted by extended family. In his old age, Grandpa retold the story until you couldn't hear it anymore—they worked him from "cain't to cain't"—from when you can't see in the morning until it's too dark to see at night. He was only able to attend school until the third grade, when he was eight years old. For the state of Alabama during his lifetime, that was sufficient for a Black child. Even if things were different, his family needed him in the fields. It wasn't a choice between school or work—it was a matter of food and survival.

The story of my grandfather's stolen childhood is far more representative of Black life in 1900 than the experience of Du Bois, who went to Harvard and became a scholar-activist, or Ida B. Wells, who graduated from Fisk and became a journalist. It's even more representative than Booker T. Washington's experience. While Washington promoted industrial education for the masses, he was an executive at an institution of higher education. And when it was time, his children didn't attend Hampton or Tuskegee. Instead, he sent his daughter to Wellesley College and Bradford Academy in Massachusetts, where she could receive a liberal arts education and have broader opportunities. That tells you something.

And still, the Black educational landscape was expanding. By 1900, more than two thousand Black people had earned higher education degrees. Most Black graduates, around 80 percent, came from HBCUs. Still, some had graduated from Harvard, Williams, Brown, Vassar, and other predominantly white institutions. And overall, the literacy rate for African Americans had risen dramatically. In 1865, at the end of the Civil War, 90 percent of Black people were illiterate. By 1900, that number had dropped to 44 percent.

So there was progress. But don't let that blind you from the real issue. While two thousand Black students had graduated from college by 1900, the population of African Americans was around nine million. At the same time, 1,751 Black lynchings had been recorded, just since 1882. That's almost one lynching for every Black college graduate in America at the time. In the South, a Black person was hanged or burned alive on average every four days between 1889 and 1929. These lynchings were carried out for "crimes" ranging from being accused of raping a white woman to something as minor as stealing a chicken, or being suspected of thinking of committing a crime.[14]

This is why industrial education alone was never going to be enough. Learning to cook, clean, and farm better wasn't going to solve the fundamental and irrational problems of systemic racism and racial terror that Black people faced.

But the debates between men like Du Bois and Washington were still crucial. They opened up space for Black people to question what kind of future we were fighting for. And those debates also became shorthand for where one stood politically. Whether one sided with Washington or Du Bois said a lot about whether the person leaned conservative or radical. These debates were important steps in our long journey toward collective freedom.

Both the work happening on the ground and the debates happening in more elite circles were essential. We needed Black people who could think and strive and dream and debate and strategize and organize and write. We also needed Black people who could build and labor and protect and pray . . . so we could stay alive.

Movements all start with ideas, with the awareness of systems of oppression, and the relentless insistence on dreaming about a radically different future. But dreaming isn't enough on its own. While Black men dominated the public discourse around Black educational futures, it was often Black women who were on the ground doing the work.

CHAPTER 4

Miss Lucy

When it comes to the history of Black education, the unsung heroes are Black women. Their labor and determination laid the foundation for hundreds of private schools across the South, especially during the harshest years of Jim Crow. While Black men like W. E. B. Du Bois and Booker T. Washington sparred in public, it was predominantly Black women—our grandmothers, great-aunties, and foremothers—who rolled up their sleeves, founded schools, educated children, and did the daily grind of liberation work. They did this work without applause; and history has done far too little to acknowledge their contributions to the ongoing battle for the Black mind.

But these women didn't operate in a vacuum. They had to navigate the deeply entangled politics of gender, class, and color. In the ongoing struggle for control over Black education, debates were not just about access but about what education for Black minds should be. Should it be public or private? Follow an industrial or liberal curricula? Reserved for the middle class, or should it aim to immediately uplift the masses?

Black women educators such as Lucy Craft Laney—the Georgia-born trailblazer whom we encountered as one of Atlanta University's first graduates—carved their paths in this contentious landscape. Their work was often against the grain—not only pushing back against white-dominated educational systems but also navigating the complex expectations placed on them within their own communities. Lucy's story is one that brings these intersections into sharp focus. Her founding of the Haines Institute in Augusta, Georgia, reveals a world of perseverance, political maneuvering, and the burden of running a private Black school in the face of systemic repression and high demands from her community.

Lucy's journey illuminates what it really took to build independent Black schools in the beginning years of Jim Crow. Through her story, we get to see how Black women, often without fanfare or support, held it down for the future of Black minds.

★ ★ ★

"Dum spiro spero" reverberated throughout the classroom as Lucy Craft Laney paced afoot, orating in Latin before her students. They'd sit up straight in awe of her presence. Short in stature, with a handsome coffee-brown face, always dressed in neat yet forgettable well-worn attire, Lucy radiated a regal air that commanded respect. "While I breathe, I hope," goes the Latin proverb. She was a living testimony of those words.

She had come a long way after earning her degree as a part of Atlanta University's inaugural class of college graduates. After a few years of working as an elementary school teacher at several Georgia public schools, she had seen enough. Miss Lucy decided to start her own school. Equipped with a college degree and her own clear vision for Black education, in 1883, Lucy opened her school in Augusta,

Georgia. She taught her first class in a lecture room located in the basement of the city's Christ Presbyterian Church. That tiny space would do just fine for that first year, as she had only five students. However, word spread like wildfire through the highways and byways of Georgia about this Black woman who was offering something different at her school—an education intended to help Black children thrive.

Miss Lucy stood out—she was a college-educated Black teacher during a time when most freedmen had only an elementary school–level education. She also had a decade of teaching experience under her belt. But what stood out most was that Miss Lucy's was a "For Us, By Us" school—established for Black children, by a Black woman. It is no surprise that by year two enrollment skyrocketed through the stratosphere, going from a literal handful of learners to 234 pupils by the next academic year—a 4,500 percent increase. Parents began sending their children to Miss Lucy from every nook and cranny of Georgia. And she desperately wanted to accept them all. However, while her educational vision for Black futures was ever abundant, her pockets were near empty. If her school was to stay afloat, she would need substantial funding to sustain it. Kids needed books and school supplies, and those who came from afar needed food, clothing, and boarding. She needed to make payroll for the rapidly expanding faculty and staff who cared for the children and the school grounds. The funding needs were endless. As a result, Lucy transformed her role from a dedicated teacher into a relentless fundraiser.

It took her almost two days to get to Minneapolis. Each time she changed trains, empty seats became harder to come by. However, she was determined to make a plea for her school. The 98th General Assembly of the Presbyterian Church convened thousands of clergy, missionaries, and church leaders to discuss the aims of the organization. With no place to freshen up before the meeting, musty and stale, Lucy went straight from the train station to the conference. Head nodding from exhaustion and travel fatigue, she waited patiently for the conference panel on "Negro Education." *"Dum spiro spero,"* she whispered to herself as she waited on the hard wooden church pew. Dreams and hopes were all she could afford to bring with her. She didn't even have the money for a return ticket.

When it was finally her turn, she took the stage to make a heart-felt appeal to the majority white audience for them to consider financially supporting her school. She had established herself as a visionary educator and leader. She also asked for alms on her own behalf to pay for her train fare back to Augusta. While she found immediate success with the latter, it appeared that her ultimate mission was a failure. She returned home empty-handed.

Francina Haines contacted Miss Lucy by phone a few weeks after the assembly. She introduced herself as the president of the Women's Mission Department of the Presbyterian Church. She called to share the news that she and her organization would both like to donate to her school. Soon after, an envelope from New Jersey containing a $10,000 check arrived in the mail. For this act of kindness and divine intervention, Miss Lucy named her school after her first major donor: the Haines Normal and Industrial Institute. Chartered in 1886 in post-Reconstruction era Augusta, Haines was officially in business as a private school for African American children.

Donations from wealthy white northerners continued over the years, although they came erratically and rarely without a spectacular amount of begging and performance on Miss Lucy's part. In addition to the Presbyterian Church, wealthy northerners such as Alice Wheeler and Caroline Phelps Stokes, both white women from New

York, donated the seed capital necessary for Lucy to build out the infrastructure for Haines's campus. Ironically, it would be the same Mrs. Stokes who would later establish the menacing educational philanthropy, the Phelps-Stokes Fund, that would come to haunt Miss Lucy in years to come.

Haines also received donations from African Americans, including a gift from the Black millionairess, Madam C. J. Walker. Once graduated and on their feet, Haines alumni set up "Lucy Laney Leagues" across the country, with chapters in major cities such as New York, Philadelphia, Columbus, and Chicago. In the spirit of racial uplift and linked fate, each chapter continuously raised funds for its alma mater. Soon, the Haines Normal and Industrial Institute campus covered an entire corner of the main throughway of Black Augusta.[1]

Miss Lucy's was not the only school in town. In fact, 1880s Augusta was fertile ground for the minds of Black youth. Schools abounded in this city in ways that had not yet taken hold in other Georgia metropolises. Augusta had Black schools that were public and private at the elementary, high school, and college levels.

Before Atlanta became the "Black Mecca" of Georgia, Augusta was the place to be.

Post-Reconstruction Black Augusta was a kaleidoscope of economics, class, and culture. It showcased the diversity of Black life and thought, and was a vibrant bubble of community and achievement.

Prior to the coming of the southern railroad, this port city nestled on the Savannah River opened the otherwise landlocked state to interstate commerce.

Industry and commerce rebounded almost immediately after the Civil War, as the city was largely spared from the fire and brimstone brought on by the Union army. With the capture of Georgia's other port city of Savannah, Union General Sherman—the same man who was initially carried out the "forty acres and a mule" presidential executive order—saw no need to bring Augusta to scorched earth. It was clear that the Union Army had won. As a result of its uninterrupted economic prosperity, Black Augustans made great strides in freedom. They worked as laborers in cotton mills and woodworks factories, as porters, longshoremen, and buggy chauffers. They were preachers, teachers, and midwives.

The city even had a class of wealthy African Americans. A vestige of slavery, the upper echelon mainly consisted of fair-skinned Blacks of mixed-race descent. Some families lived in Augusta as free people of color during slavery and enjoyed many of the same privileges and comforts as landowning whites before and after Emancipation.

Amanda America Dickson was one such person. One of the wealthiest Black Americans of the nineteenth century, she lived her life as a socialite. Her enviable wardrobe exuded elegance and stature, and she did not disappoint the discerning crowd of movers and shakers when she appeared on the scene. She was but one of several wealthy Black Augustans.[2]

Despite Jim Crow laws that excluded Black Americans from fully participating in national life, Augusta also became home to some of the most prosperous Black-owned businesses in the South. In 1898, Solomon Walker and his brother Thomas, alongside friends Walter Hornsby and J. C. Collier, pulled together the twenty-five dollars required to charter a benevolence society. Using the money earned during his time serving in the Spanish-American War, Solomon made consistent investments in the business, $2.50 at a time, until the charter was paid in full. Once licensed, the Pilgrim Health and Life Insurance Company became the first Black-owned life insurance company in the state of Georgia.

Mary McLeod Bethune and Eleanor Roosevelt at the opening of Midway Hall, May 1943. (*Courtesy National Archives, photo no.162-PBA-10-F-5612*)

Mary McLeod Bethune with a line of girls from the school in 1905. (*Photo courtesy of the State Archives of Florida*)

Starting a new building. Tuskegee student masons laying the foundation in brick. (*From The New York Public Library, https://digitalcollections.nypl.org/items/510d47de-1cef-a3d9-e040-e00a18064a99*)

Booker T. Washington and supporters. (*The Tuskegee University Archives, Tuskegee University*)

Carte-de-visite of a Freedmen's School with students and teachers. (*Collection of the Smithsonian National Museum of African American History and Culture*)

Mary McLeod Bethune, circa the 1930s. (*Scurlock Studio Records, Archives Center, National Museum of American History, Smithsonian Institution*)

W. E. B. Du Bois, Atlanta University, 1909. (*W. E. B. Du Bois Papers, Robert S. Cox Special Collections and University Archives Research Center, UMass Amherst Libraries*)

Hampton University students learning dressmaking at Hampton University, c. 1900. (*Frances Benjamin Johnston Collection Division of the Library of Congress, Washington, DC*)

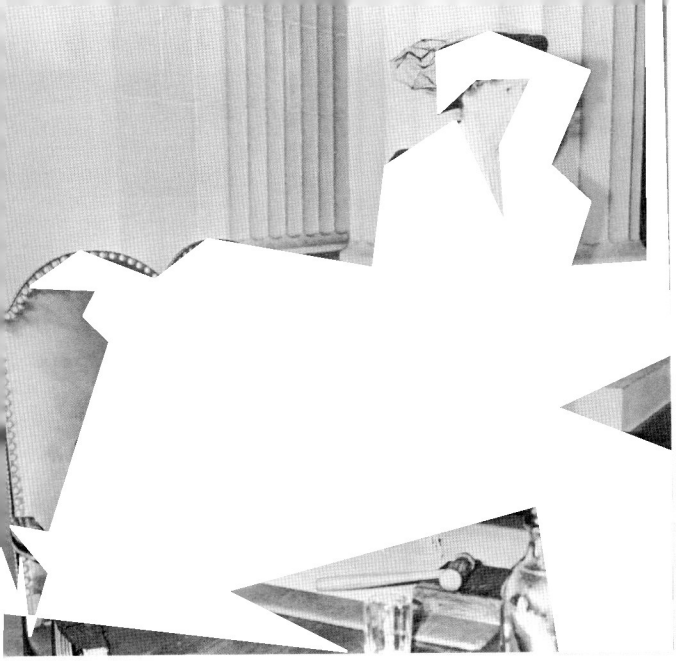

Mary McLeod Bethune and Eleanor Roosevelt speaking before an N.Y.A. meeting. (*Farm Security Administration – Office of War Information Photograph Collection Division of the Library of Congress, Washington, DC*)

Tuskegee Institute faculty with Andrew Carnegie, Tuskegee, Alabama. (*Frances Benjamin Johnston Collection Division of the Library of Congress, Washington, DC*)

Kindergarten at Haines Normal and Industrial Institute, Augusta, Georgia. (*African American Photographs Assembled for 1900 Paris Exposition Collection Division of the Library of Congress, Washington, DC*)

Sewing class at Haines Normal and Industrial Institute, Augusta, Georgia. (*African American Photographs Assembled for 1900 Paris Exposition Collection Division of the Library of Congress, Washington, DC*)

Kindergarten at Haines Normal and Industrial Institute, Augusta, Georgia (*African American Photographs Assembled for 1900 Paris Exposition Collection Division of the Library of Congress, Washington, DC*)

Cadets at Haines Normal and Industrial Institute, Augusta, Georgia. (*African American Photographs Assembled for 1900 Paris Exposition Collection Division of the Library of Congress, Washington, DC*)

Booker T. Washington giving his "Atlanta Compromise" speech. (*Alabama Department of Archives and History*)

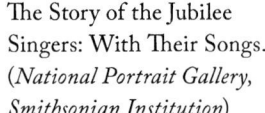

The Story of the Jubilee Singers: With Their Songs. (*National Portrait Gallery, Smithsonian Institution*)

Mary McLeod Bethune with members of the Southeastern Federation of Colored Women's Clubs (SFCWC). (*Courtesy of the Bethune–Cookman University Archives, Bethune-Cookman University, Daytona Beach, FL*)

Dr. Charlotte Hawkins Brown addressing students in the Alice Freeman Palmer building, 1947. (*Photo courtesy of North Carolina State Historic Sites*)

Photograph of Atlanta University's faculty, 1905. Photograph includes Mr. and Mrs Alonzo Herndon, W. E. B. DuBois, and George Towns. (*Atlanta University Photographs Collection, Atlanta University Center Robert W. Woodruff Library*)

Mary Smith Peake, c. 1860. (*Collection of the Hampton University Museum, Hampton, VA*)

The firm's grand five-story commercial brick building was in the epicenter of the city's Black business district. The "Golden Blocks," spanning Gwinnett and Campbell Streets, was dripping in Black business and culture.[3] Storefronts of service stations, ice cream parlors, tailors, shoemakers, and funeral homes galore lined this busy corridor in downtown Augusta. For the betting man or woman, the Del Mar Casino was always an option for a place to further circulate the Black dollar. Jobs at businesses like Pilgrim Life Insurance sustained a strong Black middle class in Augusta well into the twentieth century. Located squarely at the intersection of the Golden Blocks was the Haines Institute campus.

But Haines was not the only school in town. The mighty institution of higher learning we know today as Morehouse College also had humble beginnings in Augusta. Forty young men gathered in the basement of Springfield Baptist Church in 1867. William Jefferson White, a man who could pass as white but chose to live his life as a proud Black man, had just founded the Augusta Theological Institute. There he brought to life his vision to prepare Black men for careers in ministry and teaching. With a curriculum rooted in theology and pedagogical philosophy, the institute aimed to cultivate the next generation of "race men," a term used to describe Black people who intentionally dedicate their lives to uplifting their race. This mindset goes beyond individual success, to the overall betterment of the Black community.

By 1879, the school moved to Atlanta's Friendship Baptist Church and changed its name to Atlanta Baptist College; soon it settled into its permanent home on land in Atlanta's historic West End, donated by philanthropist John D. Rockefeller. Constructed on land that was once a bloodied Civil War battlefield, the institute's campus, designed with red brick classroom buildings, clustered dormitories, an illustrious chapel, and sprawling green grass, stood as a symbol of Black excellence.

In 1890, the college expanded its curriculum and began nurturing leaders for all facets of American life. The school's faculty was now equipped to train not only Black male teachers and preachers but also scientists, accountants, economists, and writers. In 1913, John Hope, the school's first African American president, renamed the institution Morehouse College in honor of Henry L. Morehouse, corresponding secretary of the National Baptist Home Missionary Society. Hailing from Augusta himself, President Hope, too, had sat in Lucy Craft Laney's classroom as a young boy. While Augusta's foremost Black college moved for reasons to do with space and expansion, its high school disappeared under a much more salacious set of circumstances.

Ware High School was the first public high school for African Americans in Georgia. Founded in Augusta in 1880, the school's first principal, a Black man named Richard R. Wright, named the school after the beloved Freedmen's Bureau Education superintendent and Atlanta University president, Edmund Asa Ware. Unlike most segregated public schools in the South that were forced to adopt a curriculum that mirrored the Hampton-Tuskegee model of industrial education, Ware High School embraced a liberal education model. This bold defiance of norms was a testament to the Black community's determination to ensure that Augusta's Black youth had access to a comprehensive education all the way through.

Ware's hallways echoed with a symphony of the laughter, ambition, and angst typical of any group of teenagers navigating the whirlwind of high school. The student body comprised mostly of children from middle class, elite, and fare-complexioned Black families who could afford the modest tuition. They were being groomed to become the next "talented tenth"—the upper echelon of Black Americans expected to carry the mantle of racial uplift. Ware's curriculum was preparing their minds for a life of leadership, intellectual pursuit, and racial uplift. However, as a public school funded partially by tax dollars, Ware High fell under the purview of the county board of education—an entanglement that would soon prove perilous.

When Ware opened its doors, just three years after the Compromise of 1877 had dismantled Reconstruction, Jim Crow's long arm already had Black Augusta in a chokehold. Dwindling were the days where proxies such as wealth or class afforded a Black person special protections. Augusta had its share of prosperous Black elites, like Black millionaire Amanda America Dickson, who had inherited a grand estate. Her wealth and light skin had once afforded her a sense of separation from the harsh realities faced by poorer, often darker-skinned Black residents. Now, Jim Crow laws cut through those distinctions. Racial segregation, enforced by residential covenants, drove her and other wealthy Black families out of previously integrated neighborhoods, pushing them to the other side of the railroad tracks, both literally and figuratively. No longer could their wealth or proximity to whiteness buy the privileges they once could. In the eyes of Jim Crow, they were just as Black as the poorest sharecropper.

Anti-Black racism came for Ware High School too, and by the close of the century, less than two decades from its opening, its doors were closed forever.

The blow was as swift as it was cruel. The all-white county board of education voted to defund Ware High School. The decision sent shockwaves through the Black community. As the only public high school in all of Georgia, Ware High was a sanctuary of learning and social mobility. Black parents were thrust into an emotional storm of disbelief and anger, as the school's abrupt closure felt like a death knell.

Three Black men—John W. Cummings, James S. Harper, and John C. Ladeveze—came together to fight this injustice on behalf of their community.

In 1897, these upstanding taxpaying citizens brought the battle to the courts and sued the Richmond County Board of Education. Long before *Brown v. Board of Education*, there was *Cummings v. Richmond County Board of Education*. As the case climbed through the local and state courts, and eventually up to the US Supreme Court, hope began to replenish in the community. However, it would be short-lived.

This case was one of the few early instances where the US Supreme Court reviewed racial discrimination in education. When the ruling came down in 1899, the community and three coplaintiffs' hearts sank to the depths of their souls. The Supreme Court upheld the board's actions, with the majority decision ruling that "states have the power to regulate the Negro in the enjoyment of his civil and social rights in accordance with tradition and custom, and unless his rights are greatly abused, he has no cause of complaint." The court went a step further, emphasizing that "the state need not provide for his education unless it sees fit."[4]

The defeat was more than a legal loss. Ware's closure and the prolonged legal battle morally devastated members of Augusta's Black elite. They felt as though the rug had been pulled from under them, and the social world they once knew and trusted had been violated.

Ware's closure meant that not one tax dollar would go to supporting a high school for Black Augustans, while there existed three public high schools for white kids. Time and time again, the state abdicated its responsibility to provide accessible education to Black youth. Black citizens were paying into a tax base that funded white schools yet not their own. In this way, Black Augustans were forced into participating in their own oppression.

Amid the heartbreak, some Black middle-class families chose to leave Augusta, and their identity, altogether. Ladeveze moved his family to Los Angeles, where he lived the remainder of his life passing as a white man. Another coplaintiff relocated to Philadelphia, also choosing to cash in on his complexion and leave the world on the other side of the veil behind.

By 1900, Ware High School was gone. Paine Institute, the other Black school offering high school–level courses, evolved into a college. And Augusta Theological Institute moved to Atlanta and transformed into Morehouse College. As a result, Haines Institute was the *only* high school for African Americans in the city of Augusta. It remained that way for the next forty years.

The story of Ware High School illuminates the complexities of Black life under Jim Crow. However, while some Black Augustans fought valiantly for the government to deliver on its promise to provide equality, liberty, and justice for all American citizens, others like Lucy Craft Laney did not think it time well spent trying to force white America to do right by Black children. She chose to do it herself by refusing state funding and keeping her school private.

With unyielding resolve, Miss Lucy fared the troubled waters of the ideological battle between industrial and liberal education, the choice between public versus private schools, and the long-standing tensions rooted in class and color within the Black community. She endured internal conflict with other Black leaders in Augusta, most of whom were men that resented her influence as a woman in a position of power. One of her low-key yet persistent rivals was Reverend Charles T. Walker, a fellow Black Augustan and ardent Booker T. Washington ally. Walker ran an elementary school out of his church, competing with Miss Lucy's school for resources and support from northern white donors. On more than one occasion she discovered that Walker had used his connection with Washington to steer donations away from Haines Institute toward his own school, the Walker Baptist Institute.

She also faced the never-ending challenge of courting wealthy donors who would support her vision for Black minds.

Yet, Haines's curriculum was revolutionary. It was grounded in principles designed to cultivate intellectual curiosity and critical thinking skills. The administration was composed of an all-Black faculty who taught courses in English, Latin, Greek, mathematics, sociology, literature, music, biology, US and African American history, and an array of other advanced courses—subjects that would rival the offerings of many present-day baccalaureate high schools. But Miss Lucy didn't stop there. She refused to turn her nose up to practical training. In addition to classes in the liberal arts, Haines offered vocational courses in agriculture, carpentry, cosmetology, and bookkeeping. Haines Normal and Industrial Institute embodied a motto held dear by many Black schools at the turn of the century: "Heads, Hands, Hearts." Miss Lucy was determined that every Haines graduate would leave with all three fully attended to.

From a primary school located in a church basement with five students, Miss Lucy grew Haines into the first Black kindergarten and Black nursing school in Augusta. And when Ware High School closed, Haines was the only Black high school in the city. The footprint of campus included buildings full of classrooms, dormitories for boys and girls, a library, a chapel, and a football field. Extracurricular clubs included a traveling debate team and chorus.

The "who's who" of arts, politics, and industry made sure to visit and give talks at Haines when passing through Georgia, including notable figures such as scholar-activist W. E. B. Du Bois; writer, artist, and civil rights leader James Weldon Johnson; the twenty-seventh president of the United States, William Howard Taft; and world reknowned opera singer Marion Anderson.

In addition to expanding and stewarding Haines, Lucy served as a mentor and role model to the next generation of Black school founders.

★ ★ ★

March 26th, 1911[5]

Dear Dr. Du Bois:-

Do you know anyone who will help us? I want to raise $3,000 to get out of debt. This amount will make me even with the world.

I had hoped to raise it here among the tourists but. Dr. Washington came and rallied all the moneygiving people for Tabernacle Church and Walker Institute. I was so unfortunate several years ago to incur the displeasure of Dr. Washington—since then he has not allowed anyone to give us money. He stopped Mr. Converse and Mr. Carnegie from helping us and prevented Miss Stokes from giving what she had led me to believe she would give. Mr. Walker and Floyd also had my paper refused 2nd class rate.

I am not complaining and would rather nothing be paid of this, I don't like to mention it, and do so now only in confidence. I sorely need help at once.

Sincerely,

L. C. Laney

Lucy's hand trembled with quiet rage as she penned the letter to the good doctor W. E. B. Du Bois. A prideful woman with deeply ingrained Christian values, Lucy seldom took to speaking ill of others, but Du Bois was a trusted friend and collaborator. He had suffered his own issues with Booker T. Washington. The Atlanta University Studies was the only systematic sociological study of the social and economic conditions of the American Negro in the South, a program led by Du Bois for over a decade. In reflecting on his struggles during that era in his life, he wrote about how he struggled to keep his research program going due to what he believed was a similar kind of sabotage by Washington. While Du Bois was able to sympathize with Lucy, he couldn't help her because he, too, was blackballed by the Tuskegee Machine.

By the time Lucy sent him her letter, he had resigned his university position and joined the National Association for the Advancement of Colored People as director of research and served as editor in chief of *The Crisis* magazine. He gave up on his belief that he could dismantle white racism by showing through facts, data, and evidence that Black people were not inherently inferior. He embraced the fact that racism is violent and irrational. However, he did not give up on his commitment to Black liberation; he just decided that he could have more impact by focusing on uplifting the Black masses through *The Crisis* instead of trying to convince white people to give up their racism.[6]

Lucy had poured her heart into the Haines Institute. Through all the turmoil and changing political tides, her high school was the last one standing in Augusta. Her decision not to accept tax dollars protected her school from having its fate in the hands of the all-white county board of education. As we saw in the case of Ware High School, this could put her school at risk of being shut down.

Instead, she insisted on maintaining full autonomy over Haines and its curriculum. It also meant that she was solely responsible for keeping the lights on—paying teacher and staff salaries, acquiring land and erecting new buildings, buying books and supplies, and all the other expenses that come with running a school.

Miss Lucy was staring up a mountain.

Booker T. Washington's ability to control the flow of white dollars to Black institutions meant that any perceived personal slight against him could unknowingly leave them blacklisted. There was little room for Black progress in education that did not align with his views. Miss Lucy's national accolades and successful graduates were not enough to shield her from his wrath.

Black intellectuals like Du Bois championed the work she was doing, but a school cannot survive on hope, notoriety, and moral support alone.[7] She traveled the country appealing to the consciousness of wealthy individuals and philanthropies in hopes that they would donate just one more dollar to keep Haines alive. Although she held the confidence and favor of many of the wealthiest families in the country, including the Rockefellers and the Carnegies, no donor ever simply endowed Miss Lucy's school. Instead, she lived a life of robbing Peter to pay Paul.

Lucy Craft Laney died exhausted and with few material possessions to her name. And not long after her last breath, the hope of Haines Normal and Industrial Institute soon passed on with her. Unfortunately, Miss Lucy's story is also that of many Black school founders of the Jim Crow era.

CHAPTER 5

Lifting as We Climb

As a Black educator and intellectual, when I set out to accomplish something—whether it's preparing for a keynote speech, writing a book, or filming for a documentary—I cannot think of a time when I've ever done it alone. I'm always deeply aware and grateful that I move in a community. I am a product of their collective wisdom and genius.

Every day, I feel the presence of the giants whose shoulders I stand on—my ancestors and elders who paved the way. But just as important, on a daily basis, my ability to keep going and to reach for higher heights is because I am locked in arm in arm with my support system—my people.

The thousand things I have going on are almost always made possible by the strength, encouragement, and insight from the wise counsel I keep in my corner. These are the folks who share my vision or simply want to see me win—each of them out here making moves in their own respective worlds. In writing this book alone, I've relied on countless writing retreats, listening sessions, late-night phone calls, encouraging texts, and people who sat with me while I talked myself off a ledge. Tapping into the deep knowledge I needed to bring this book out required all that support. And honestly, that's what always gets me through, no matter what I'm working on.

This kind of community support isn't unique to me. It's part of the ethos of the Black American experience. Historically, Black folks have *had* to do things collectively. We've built and sustained one another, knowing that for better or worse, our fates are linked. It's that idea that you're working on something bigger than yourself—an understanding woven into the fabric of African American culture.

For me, this sense of community was instilled from an early age. I come from a big family—twenty-five aunts and uncles across both sides, and over forty cousins—all of us growing up together within a five-mile radius. That feeling of being part of a collective was just a fact of life. It extended to our family's institutions too, especially the church. At Faith Baptist Church, where my family raised me, you didn't just show up; you showed out. I sang in the choir and served on the usher board—my parents pressed that sense of collective responsibility on me from the start. The lesson was clear: To be part of something bigger than yourself, you must be present and contribute.

Learning to see your aims and visions as part of a collective good, rather than just for individual gain, was a lesson I absorbed early on. It wasn't just my immediate family or my church that taught me this— our whole extended family lived it. Take our family reunions down south, for instance. Someone would always organize the T-shirts; others would be on the cooking squad—some frying fish, others manning the grill. Everything about it, even down to the logistics, was a practice in collective effort. So, when I stepped into the world as a young adult, carrying these sensibilities came naturally to me.

When I got to graduate school at Brown University, where I earned my PhD in sociology, I found myself in an environment on the brink of uprising. At that time, the department faculty was almost entirely white, while more than half of the graduate students were Black and brown. The disconnect was clear to us students of color, and we organized among ourselves to push to diversify the faculty. We wanted instructors who could bring culturally relevant pedagogy, who could speak to the issues impacting our lives, and who would support the kinds of research we were passionate about. It wasn't just for us as individuals—it was about creating an academic community that could serve future students as well. For the ethics and health of the department, we needed faculty who looked more like the world.

I understood our strength in numbers and the necessity of getting organized. This same ethos was even more prevalent back in the early twentieth century, when Black life, especially in the South, demanded that Black people create their own safety nets, their own institutions, and their own organizations as a matter of survival. This way of rejecting hyper-individualism is deeply woven into the Black American experience, shaped by histories of exclusion and resilience.

Even though Jim Crow was alive and well—with philanthropies stirring chaos on one side and the state turning its back on Black communities on the other—Black people in the early 1900s were determined to steer their own course. They found ways to reshape their educational and social realities despite the constraints of the system. Black folks didn't just pursue avenues to be better for themselves—they organized on behalf of the entire community.

I keep returning to this concept of "racial uplift" because it was a guiding principle for so many Black Americans during this era. They saw their own advancement as part of a larger project of Black empowerment. The work wasn't done until they reached the top and could look left and right and see others who looked like them standing alongside. Black folks shared knowledge, passed along opportunities, and advocated for one another's needs. It was—and remains—a commitment to rising together.

This was what most Black people were on in those days. You saw it everywhere—Black people were building institutions and organizations across the country, creating a constellation of forces dedicated to advancing Black futures on every front. Politically, socially, economically, and especially in education, these organizations formed an ecosystem that spoke directly to the needs and dreams of Black communities. They emerged because they had to. By and large, Black people were excluded from white institutions—their churches, labor unions, sororities, fraternities, and so on. Since we couldn't have a seat at those tables, we built our own.

We created alliances so we could use our collective power to set Black agendas and push them forward. And these weren't "woe-is-me" agendas focused on what we lacked. No, these were bold, asset-based visions grounded in empowerment, dignity, and equity. Back then, we bet on Black, and we are reaping the dividends of those investments to this day.

It was a prodigious time for Black organizing. In the first two decades of the twentieth century alone, organizations like the Niagara Movement emerged as trailblazers for Black civil rights. Founded in 1905 by leaders like W. E. B. Du Bois and William Monroe Trotter, the Niagara Movement marked a bold new chapter in Black advocacy. This was an all-Black organization, started by twenty-nine men who gathered in Niagara Falls. They came together in response to Booker T. Washington's philosophy of gradual rights and accommodation, which, to them, was unacceptable.

The men of the Niagara Movement rejected gradualism and instead demanded full equality—now. They wanted full voting rights—now. They wanted equal access to education—now. They wanted an end to Jim Crow and racial violence—not tomorrow, not soon, but right now. This organization was a powerful, unyielding declaration of Black collective political organizing. In 1909, it morphed into the National Association for the Advancement of Colored People (NAACP), the multiracial organization we know today. But before that transformation, the Niagara Movement stood as a Black-led institution—an unapologetic statement of resistance and self-determination.

Black women also recognized the power of organizing around our specific needs—not just as Black people and not just as women, but as Black women. Across the country, dozens of local Black women's organizations were forming. They created mutual aid societies, savings groups, and social clubs to address the gaps left by America's social safety net. These groups empowered Black women to build community power and set agendas around issues that directly impacted their lives.

In 1896, the National Association of Colored Women's Clubs (NACWC) was founded, uniting thousands of Black women across the nation under a single purpose. Its motto, "Lifting as We Climb," perfectly embodied the ethos of racial uplift. At the helm of the NACWC were some of the most audacious and fierce Black women of the time—trailblazers like Mary Church Terrell, the organization's first president, and abolitionist and freedom fighter, Ida B. Wells. Together, they led an organization that blended community service with unflinching advocacy, uplifting the voices and needs of Black women and their communities.

One of the NACWC's core missions was to confront the damaging portrayals of Black women in society. No matter what they achieved, Black women were most often reduced to stereotypes—either as "mammies" meant to comfort and serve white needs at their own expense or as "vixens," depicted as morally loose and inferior to white women. These portrayals were insulting and were weaponized against Black women in every space they entered, from workplaces to public venues. But the NACWC didn't just play defense against these portrayals; they went on the offense, setting a vision for the world Black women wanted to see.

They asked: What does a world look like where we are affirmed, where we can stand as equals, fully human and fully respected? To answer, they advocated fiercely for Black women's suffrage, joining the broader suffrage movement with a unique perspective. Their fight wasn't just about the right to vote; it was about asserting Black women's place in public life. They also prioritized issues of education, especially access for Black women and girls.

This was a time when Black Americans weren't just creating organizations to seek refuge. We were carving out spaces to lead, learn, and advocate for ourselves. And to love ourselves.

This was also the era when Black teachers' associations began to emerge, connecting Black educators nationwide. These associations allowed them to collaborate, set agendas, and take ownership of Black education. They put the power in the hands of local Black teachers, empowering them to define what Black schools should offer and how Black children should be taught. Teachers shared strategies, tips on pedagogy, textbook recommendations, and, importantly, materials about Black history—content that was often absent from the standard curriculum or the hand-me-down textbooks sent to Black schools. Through these associations, they ensured that Black students were exposed to a fuller, richer history, one that honored their heritage and contributions to the world. Black teachers' associations were the lifeline that made this possible, the essential network through which information flowed and kept teachers unified and organized.[1]

The first national teachers' association for Black educators was founded in 1903, initially called the National Association of Negro Teachers. It would evolve into the National Association of Teachers in Colored Schools in 1907 and later become the American Teachers Association in 1937. For decades, these associations amplified the voices of Black educators. They allowed teachers to share strategies, confront challenges head-on, and unify around a common purpose. Part of what organizing does is force clarity—clarity on your agenda, on who you are, and on what you stand for. Is this about civic engagement? Advancement? Access? Pedagogy? Once that clarity is there, you can define what victory looks like. These early teachers' associations were setting that vision, doing the work of radical imagination that any social movement requires—the audacity to envision something better.

And it wasn't just national organizations. There were dozens of Black teachers' associations at every level—county, regional, statewide—and they all fed into the broader national network. Black educators were often affiliated with multiple organizations simultaneously, creating a web of information sharing. And as we know, knowledge is power. These networks opened the floodgates, allowing Black educators and parents to get on the same page.

Amid all this organizing, an extraordinary alliance was forming. You can think of it as the archenemy of the Tuskegee Machine: an informal coalition of Black women educators who would become the matriarchs of Black education. Black women formed this shared sisterhood, for a few reasons. For one, the teaching profession was overwhelmingly feminized. While Black men often held principal positions, Black women made up most of the teaching staff.[2] They were the ones on the front lines in the classroom, shaping young minds. For this reason, their alliances and power building were uniquely vital to the battle for the Black mind.

Black women educators of this era went far beyond teaching. They were school founders, institution builders, and visionaries. Following the trail blazed by pioneers like Lucy Craft Laney, a new generation of Black women grabbed the baton, founding schools and establishing networks that would sustain them and their work. Despite competing for the same private funds, they understood their power lay in sisterhood. These women joined forces with other Black women educators, teachers, school founders, and parents, forming a united front that pushed against the limitations of Jim Crow and championed the cultivation of Black minds.

In contrast to the Tuskegee Machine, they crafted an educational machine of their own—one fueled by sisterhood, resilience, and an unyielding commitment to Black self-determination.

They gathered to discuss academics and explore what it meant to educate the whole Black child, to raise a generation with a sense of pride, joy, and dignity, despite a society that constantly told them they should have none of those things. They leaned into the "head, hands, and heart" model—intellectual enrichment, practical skill building, and emotional and spiritual empowerment. These educators aimed to prepare Black children for the unique challenges they would face as Black people in America. They were shaping a Black self-image, fostering an identity rooted in their own definition of who they were rather than the one imposed on them by a society determined to belittle their worth.

Lucy Craft Laney, who founded the Haines Institute in Augusta in 1883, was one of the first. Back then, she was navigating uncharted waters in a hostile landscape—the rise of Jim Crow, which was the post-Reconstruction crackdown on Black progress. She stood alone, establishing her school without the backing of organized networks, national institutions, or the resources that came with them. There was no blueprint for what she was doing. Laney and her contemporaries had to create something out of nothing, fueled only by their own will, faith, ingenuity, and, sometimes, local community support. Hers was a time when even the idea of widespread Black education still seemed out of reach.

By the early twentieth century, the seeds they had sown had blossomed, sustained by a critical mass of educated Black folks. Black schools had now graduated generations of students, many of whom went on to higher education at historically Black colleges and universities and, eventually, even some predominantly white institutions in the North. With this new crop of college-educated Black people, the capacity for organized power grew.

This collective progress birthed a new era. Black communities could now organize on a larger scale—not only advancing education but fueling the broader Black freedom struggle. The battle for the Black mind was, and has always been, inextricably linked with the broader fight for liberation. Education has always been central—not only for feeding our minds but as a space for Black power building and collective vision setting, and as an incubator for the Black freedom struggle.

Many of the organizations that rose to champion Black rights, dignity, and civil rights found their roots on college campuses. These were spaces where students gathered, debated, and dreamed. Young people have always been at the heart of change—bold enough to insist on a new way of being, daring enough to build a better world.

In classrooms and dorm rooms, on campuses across the country, a new generation of Black youth came into their own, equipped with the skills, knowledge, and networks to shape their destinies.

Together, they formed alliances, drawing inspiration from educators and mentors who saw their potential and who gave them the space—and the runway—to take flight.

These young people organized clubs, debate teams, and study groups. They engaged in spirited discussions about America's future, justice, and liberation. United by a shared purpose, Black students and teachers fought to transcend the limitations imposed on them, creating spaces where Black lives and Black minds could thrive.

Black sororities and fraternities—known today as the Divine Nine—are a powerful example of this legacy. They began as sanctuaries of support and pride for Black college students navigating predominantly white institutions. In 1906, Alpha Phi Alpha, the first intercollegiate Black Greek-letter organization, was founded by seven Black male students at Cornell University. These young men knew they needed a space for themselves as Black men in a mostly white academic world, and they found strength in brotherhood.

Black women soon followed. In 1908, nine juniors and seniors founded Alpha Kappa Alpha Sorority at Howard University, marking the beginning of a legacy of Black sisterhood, excellence, and service. A few years later, in 1913, Delta Sigma Theta emerged, also on Howard's campus. Twenty-two Black women, committed to public service and civic engagement, founded the sorority—and marched boldly in the historic 1913 women's suffrage parade in Washington, DC. They took a stand for Black women's right to vote and to participate fully in civic life.

This was the world the next generation of Black teachers stepped into. Unlike Lucy Craft Laney, these teachers were not alone. They were part of a vibrant, interconnected network of Black educators and leaders who supported and uplifted one another. This alliance was beyond coincidence; it was intentional.

Many of these educators had cut their teeth in the NACWC, as education was the cornerstone of the organization's mission. Prominent figures like Mary Church Terrell, Harriet Tubman, and journalist and anti-lynching activist Ida B. Wells-Barnett helped shape its vision.

Within this coalition, Black women made waves across the nation—each a force in her own right. They were educators, activists, founders, and organizers who saw education as both a right and a pathway to liberation.

Nannie Helen Burroughs, for example, was born in 1879 and would go on to establish the National Training School for Women and Girls in Washington, DC, in 1909. Her school emphasized vocational training and moral development for Black women, empowering them to achieve economic independence. Burroughs was also active in the NACW and the National Baptist Convention, championing women's rights within religious spaces. Margaret Murray Washington, the wife of Booker T. Washington, was another trailblazer. A dedicated educator, she cofounded the NACW and played a pivotal role in shaping the Tuskegee Institute, tirelessly advocating for education and social services for Black communities.[3]

Mary Church Terrell, one of the first Black women to earn a college degree in the United States, was both a charter member of the NAACP and a founding member of the NACW. Her life's work was a campaign against racial and gender discrimination, and she used her platform to uplift the importance of education. There was also Anna Julia Cooper, born in 1858, an educator and scholar who became the first Black woman to earn a PhD at the Sorbonne in France. Her influential book, *A Voice from the South*, called for the education of Black women as essential to the uplift of the whole race. As the head of the M Street High School in Washington,

DC, she set high academic standards, preparing Black students for higher education.[4]

Together, these women and their organizations created networks of support and systems of advocacy, addressing the systemic challenges Black communities faced. And they were doing so largely outside the public school system. Their institutions were Black private schools, spaces they controlled, with curricula and missions tailored to what they believed aligned with the needs and aspirations of their communities.

While Black private schools didn't represent the majority of schools available to Black children, they broadened the landscape of educational choices, giving Black families alternatives to the rigid industrial education model imposed by the Hampton-Tuskegee system.

Let's take a closer look at two schools—founded by two remarkable women: Mary McLeod Bethune and Charlotte Hawkins Brown—that illustrate the diversity within this constellation.

★ ★ ★

Born in 1875, during Reconstruction, Mary McLeod was one of the few in her family to be born free. Being the fifteenth of seventeen children, she understood the weight of opportunity in ways her older siblings never got the chance to. And she didn't waste it.

She excelled in school, attending a local missionary school where her teacher, a white woman named Emma J. Wilson, saw her potential. Wilson helped secure her a scholarship to Scotia Seminary for Negro Girls in North Carolina. This was where Mary's world expanded. At Scotia, she was immersed in a Christian education that tied religious values to learning, and she had the rare experience of studying in an all-girls environment, allowing her to focus on her intellectual growth without the usual pressures of gendered expectations.

After Scotia, she spent a year at Moody Bible Institute in Chicago, with dreams of becoming a missionary in Africa. But at the time, white missionary organizations had become increasingly weary of Black Americans stirring up ideas of freedom and resistance among native Africans, so she was denied the opportunity and had to shift gears.

Instead of going abroad, she spent a year apprenticing with the legendary Lucy Craft Laney at Haines Institute in Augusta, Georgia. During that year of training, Lucy taught Mary the ropes of owning a school—from curriculum design to scouting an ideal location to fundraising. In 1898, Mary returned to her hometown in South Carolina and married Albertus Bethune.

Mary McLeod Bethune was a tour de force. She dedicated her life to building opportunities for Black girls who were too often overlooked. In 1904, she and her husband moved from their hometown in South Carolina to Daytona Beach, Florida, where she set out to take the first step in fulfilling her life's purpose. With only $1.50 in her purse, she opened the Daytona Normal and Industrial Institute for Negro Girls in a small, rented room. From the beginning, she was strategic. To attract support, she emphasized the school's practical goals, highlighting subjects like English, arithmetic, and Bible study. But for Bethune, the school's true mission was so much deeper than what was presented on the report card.

Bethune envisioned Daytona Institute as a sanctuary and a launchpad for Black girls—a place where they could cultivate the skills and resilience they would need to thrive in a world hostile to their existence. She was determined to show the world that Black girls were more than the roles society had laid out for them. They were leaders, thinkers, activists, and the backbone of their communities. Bethune believed in the power of education to prepare her students for a life as Black women in America, facing the unique challenges that came with that identity. In her essay, "A Philosophy of Education for Negro Girls," she wrote, "Negro women have always known struggle," and she taught her students with that in mind. Bethune's curriculum was infused with what she called "the zeal of struggle"—preparing her students not only to survive but to live with pride, strength, and purpose.[5]

And she wasn't afraid to make tough decisions along the way. Her marriage to Albertus lasted only about ten years before he left. The reasons remain unclear, but what we do know is that after he was gone, Mary referred to herself as a widow—even though Albertus was alive and well back in South Carolina. She raised their son, Albert, on Daytona Institute's campus, and despite her personal sacrifices, she remained undeterred from her mission. Like so many Black women educators of her time—including her mentor Lucy Craft Laney—Bethune found that personal relationships often took a back seat to her work. The weight of her purpose, and the societal resistance she faced as a Black woman with power, strained many of her relationships. But Bethune, like the women before her, kept pushing forward.

Her work at Daytona became legendary, but her impact went far beyond the classroom. Bethune was also a formidable political leader, uniting Black women through education-based organizations. She served as president of the Florida Federation of Colored Women's Clubs, founded a home for delinquent Black girls in Ocala, and led the twelve-state Southeastern Federation of Colored Women's Clubs. Through these networks, she built powerful alliances, pooling resources and setting agendas that addressed the specific needs of Black women and children. Her influence was so profound that she was often seen as the "female Booker T. Washington," a title that recognized her pragmatic, hands-on approach to education and leadership.

But while Washington focused on accommodation, Bethune had a bold, unflinching commitment to integration and civil rights.

Throughout her life, Bethune remained committed to the ideal of American democracy. Unlike Washington, who avoided pushing against segregation and disenfranchisement, Bethune was all in on integration and civil rights. She believed that Black people were not outsiders clawing their way into American society; they were an essential part of it, with every right to full participation. In Daytona, she led voter registration efforts for Black citizens, even in the face of Ku Klux Klan intimidation.[6] The Klan showed up on her campus more than once, but she refused to be silenced. For her, voting was a sacred right and a nonnegotiable part of the struggle for freedom. Bethune's vision was for Black people to take their rightful place at the table of American society, to be present in every sphere, from politics to education to business. She was as unapologetically Black as she was unapologetically American.

In the later years of her life, that dedication took her all the way to the White House, where she advised two US presidents on issues affecting Black Americans. She knew that American democracy could not truly be realized until Black people were recognized, respected, and fully included.

★ ★ ★

Charlotte Hawkins Brown's early life looked very different from Mary McLeod Bethune's. Yet both women found themselves as educational entrepreneurs around the same time, navigating the challenges of the Jim Crow South. Despite their different beginnings, they became friends and collaborated at various points in their careers, though their visions for Black educational futures diverged in some ways.[7]

Charlotte was born in Henderson, North Carolina, in 1883. When she was still a child, her family moved north to Cambridge, Massachusetts, where she spent most of her formative years. Growing up in Massachusetts gave Charlotte access to opportunities that were rare for Black children in America at that time. She attended Boston English High, one of the country's first public high schools, and experienced a multiracial, coeducational learning environment that most Black children in the South could only dream of.

Toward the end of her high school years, a chance encounter would change the course of her life. While walking and babysitting a child, Charlotte was reading Virgil—a Latin classic—when she caught the attention of Alice Freeman Palmer, a white woman who was then the president of Wellesley College. Impressed by the sight of a young Black girl engrossed in such an advanced text, Palmer stopped to talk to her. That conversation sparked a relationship that eventually helped Charlotte gain entry to Salem State University in Massachusetts. But before she could graduate, Charlotte was approached by the AMA with a life-changing proposition: to return to North Carolina and become the principal of a small Black rural school.

Charlotte took the leap, packing her bags and heading back south. She arrived in Sedalia, North Carolina—a tiny rural community outside Greensboro—by leaping off a slowing train, suitcases in hand, as there was no train station in her new home. This literal leap of faith would become emblematic of her life story. Initially, she ran the Bethany Institute under the AMA's leadership, but the religious organization closed the school within a year of her arrival due to financial troubles. She found herself facing another life-defining choice: return to Cambridge or stay in Sedalia and build a school. She chose to stay.

Over the next fifty years, Charlotte transformed her school from a small, rural industrial school into an internationally recognized finishing school, known for preparing the next generation of Black elites. The Palmer Memorial Institute was a self-contained boarding school where Black students lived and learned together. The curriculum was designed not just for academic excellence but to teach these students how to carry themselves with the polish, confidence, and sophistication required for high society. This was a school for the future upper echelon of Black America, and Charlotte took the job of shaping them seriously.

Palmer's curriculum went beyond the basics. Charlotte's New England upbringing influenced her emphasis on social graces, etiquette, and self-presentation—values that were all but foreign to Jim Crow's southern rigidity. But in the confines of Palmer Institute's campus, senior girls moved into a small house on campus where they practiced hosting dinner parties, setting tables, and entertaining guests. The idea was to equip them with skills they would need when they graduated, married, and entered society. Charlotte was particular about how her students carried themselves. She cared about details—how Black women applied their makeup, how Black men tied their ties and wore jackets to dinner, and whether a gentleman knew to pull out a chair for a lady. Cleanliness, orderliness, punctuality, proper diction, and poise were not just encouraged; they were mandatory.[8]

Charlotte even authored a book, *The Correct Thing to Do—to Say—to Wear*, which became the standard for Palmer students. The

Palmer Institute was a boarding school where the faculty, including Charlotte, lived on campus. So there was no escaping her rules and standards. And Palmerites bonded over shared experiences—including resisting Charlotte's strict rules! But in the end, those rules shaped them into adults who embodied Black excellence, and the Palmer experience left an indelible mark on their lives.[9]

Charlotte Hawkins Brown understood all too well the degrading stereotypes that plagued Black women in American society. Determined to counteract these harmful portrayals, she maintained high standards for how her female students presented themselves. She expected Palmer graduates to be walking counternarratives to these stereotypes, ensuring that in public, they would be perceived as "ladies" in every sense of the word. Even something as minor as a girl wearing too much lipstick could raise Brown's eyebrow, possibly even leading to a stern warning or, in repeated cases, a threat of expulsion.[10]

For students, the threat of being sent home was a constant, unspoken reminder to uphold Brown's standards. Families from all over the country and beyond had entrusted their children to Palmer, seeing their attendance as a source of pride and prestige. Brown used this deep-seated pride to keep her students in line, knowing that the stakes of a misstep were high—not just for the individual but for the families who had invested so much in their education.

Palmer Institute sat on four hundred acres of rural North Carolina land, a sprawling campus that not only housed classrooms but also farmland where students worked to cover tuition if needed. This arrangement reinforced Brown's values of "head, hands, and hearts" that was central to so many Black private schools at the time.

Charlotte's influence extended to every corner of campus life. Alumni recall how she knew every student's name, kept in close contact with their families, and didn't hesitate to send a child home if she felt they weren't meeting the Palmer Institute's standards. Her omnipresence and watchful eye were a defining feature of the Palmer experience.

Palmer Institute wasn't all rules and rigor, however; it also offered creative outlets and cultural education. Like many Black schools, Palmer had its own entertainment groups, including a dance troupe and the renowned Sedalia Singers choir. But while other Black school choirs often performed Negro spirituals, the Sedalia Singers specialized in classical music—Brown's preference. This repertoire served a dual purpose: it elevated Palmer's image among white benefactors, and it equipped students with the versatility to move seamlessly between cultural spaces.[11] Brown saw this as a critical skill for her graduates. She wanted them to be able to navigate a world that demanded excellence in both "Negro" and "American" cultural realms, embodying the "twoness"—the sometimes-contradictory experience of being Black and American—that W. E. B. Du Bois described in *The Souls of Black Folk*.

The Palmer curriculum nurtured this dual identity by giving students the tools to succeed in a society that often denied their humanity and rights. She wasn't trying to make her students "the good ones" to white society; rather, she was ensuring they could hold their heads high in any space, exuding the dignity and self-respect they had cultivated at Palmer.

Parents sent their children to Palmer from cities like Philadelphia, New York, Chicago, and Los Angeles, and even from places as far as Haiti, Cuba, Liberia, and Costa Rica. Palmer's reputation as a Black institution that cultivated cosmopolitanism, dignity, and refinement drew families from all walks of life. For many, the school was a haven—a place where their children could receive an education free from the racial hostility in segregated cities and communities.

Palmer's student body included the children of Black elites, such as Madam C. J. Walker's granddaughter and Martin Luther King Jr.'s younger brother, A. D. King, who attended Palmer (although he was eventually sent home for misbehavior). Even the nieces of Eslanda and Paul Robeson graced its halls. Yet Palmer was not exclusively for the wealthy; Brown also welcomed children from poorer families, allowing them to take on extra work on campus to cover their tuition.

In every aspect, Palmer Institute was a place of high expectations and strict discipline. Brown instilled in her students the idea that "you are somebody"—not just for themselves but as representatives of their race. The way they spoke, dressed, and carried themselves mattered. They were taught to embody Black excellence, a philosophy that aligned with the New Negro movement and foreshadowed the Harlem Renaissance's celebration of Black identity and culture.[12] Palmer Institute was a world within a world, a place where young Black people could practice self-respect, poise, and confidence, preparing to face a society that often denied them these very attributes.

Charlotte Hawkins Brown was a visionary, a woman who saw her role not merely as an educator but as a cultivator of Black leadership and dignity. Palmer Institute was a testament to her belief in Black pride and self-respect—a belief that despite societal limitations, Black people could set their own standards and define their own futures.

The lives and legacies of Brown and Bethune remind us that the power of Black education was never solely about individual achievements; it was always rooted in community and a broader vision for collective freedom. As products and leaders of a network of Black organizations, they and their peers understood that true progress required a network of support—sororities, teachers' associations, women's clubs, and social networks that fortified Black communities from within.

Through their schools, they offered Black families a spectrum of educational choices, each one a refuge from the limitations imposed by white society. By leaning on each other and amplifying each other's work, the matriarchs of Black education created a legacy that extended far beyond their individual classrooms. It is a powerful reminder that our strength has always been in our togetherness, in the community we build and sustain, and in the institutions we create that reflect our values, our dreams, and our collective will to "lift as we climb."

CHAPTER 6

Square Biz

When Charlotte Hawkins Brown founded Palmer Memorial Institute in 1902, the school was operated in a dilapidated shack sitting on fifteen acres of land in rural North Carolina. Within ten years, she had transformed her institution into a thriving campus spanning over four hundred acres. Mary McLeod Bethune founded her school in 1904 with just $1.50 in her pocket—and no funding in sight. Today, Bethune-Cookman University still stands and continues its legacy of educating some of the brightest Black minds. These women built lasting educational institutions that became a part of the bedrock of independent private schools from Black minds under Jim Crow. How they managed to do this, with virtually no resources and against constant opposition, is a story of pure grit and entrepreneurial genius.

Mary and Charlotte faced challenges that most of us today would find unimaginable. These weren't occasional hurdles or onetime battles; these were daily, relentless struggles that demanded their full attention, energy, and creativity. These women had to be more than educators—they had to be business moguls, strategists, and visionary leaders all at once. In addition to setting the curricula and teaching students, they were running businesses, balancing books, pitching donors, managing staff, securing land, and navigating financial audits. They were building national brands and managing every aspect of their schools' survival and growth.

At a time when tens of millions of philanthropic dollars were flowing into the ecosystem of Black education, surprisingly few of those dollars ever made it to K–12 Black schools like Palmer and Daytona Institute. Instead, Black women educators were made to survive on scraps, constantly cobbling together resources to keep their doors open. And yet, they made it happen. For Black private schools in the early 1900s, the reality was simple: make a dollar out of fifteen cents, or watch your vision fade away.

Mary and Charlotte lived by this hard truth. In a world determined to see them fail, they didn't just keep the lights on—they kept their schools open and thriving for more than half a century. This kind of endurance, ingenuity, and business savvy deserves recognition. What strategies did they employ behind the scenes to accomplish what many would have believed to be impossible?

If there's one thing these women mastered, it was the art of storytelling. In American culture, nothing tugs at the heartstrings quite like a good rags-to-riches story—the kind where someone scrapes their way up from nothing, fueled by grit, perseverance, and the drive to prove everyone wrong. It's the classic American Dream narrative, and both Charlotte and Mary knew how to work it like pros. They understood that the right origin story could turn their schools into symbols of possibility and hope, inspiring people to see them not just as mere schools but as beacons of the future.

Now, were these stories always 100 percent factual? Probably not. But that wasn't the point. The point was to craft a narrative so compelling that it bypassed logic and went straight to people's hearts. They knew how to sell the dream, tapping into that American ethos of "pull yourself up by your bootstraps" and reminding folks of the power of taking a risk and betting on oneself. They told these stories so well that people couldn't help but root for them.

Mary McLeod Bethune's origin story is iconic: with unmistakable flair, she would recount how she arrived in Daytona with nothing but a dollar and fifty cents in her pocket and a God-given vision to start a school for Black girls. It sounded like the ultimate tale of going from nothing to something, and people ate it up. Sure, she had backing from local Black churches and support from her community. And yes, she did get help from some wealthy white winter vacationers who pitched in with food, clothes, and even some furniture. But the story of that lone dollar and fifty cents hit different. It was the perfect marketing hook, and Mary knew it.

Charlotte Hawkins Brown had her own take on this classic tale. According to her, she jumped off a moving train in North Carolina at nineteen years old, suitcases in hand and no money to her name, ready to start a school in a place she barely knew. That's the kind of image that stays with you. Charlotte used this tale to great effect, especially when she was working her New England fundraising circles. It painted a picture of unshakable resolve and ambition, and folks were captivated. They understood that whether every detail was true or not didn't even matter because the spirit of story was true.

Both Mary and Charlotte knew that sometimes a story is the most effective fundraising tool in one's arsenal. After all, who can resist rooting for someone with a dream and the sheer will to bring it to life, even when the odds are stacked against them?

Mary was relentless in her pursuit of funding for her school. She wrote letter after letter to some of the wealthiest philanthropists of her time, including heavy hitters like Julius Rosenwald, Andrew Carnegie, and John Rockefeller. She even reached out to Booker T. Washington, asking him to put in a good word on her behalf. Evidence of whether these efforts directly paid off is scant, but Mary didn't let that deter her efforts. She even went so far as to write an open letter to the *New York Times*, boldly calling on everyday Americans for support. Everywhere she went, she made her case loud and clear to anyone who'd listen.

It was more than ambition that drove Mary. It was a deep, abiding love for Black girls. She knew exactly what awaited them if no one stepped in—steamy laundry rooms, hot kitchens, and faceless domestic work in white households. She could see the futures they'd be boxed into without education. But Mary saw so much more for their lives. She saw brilliance. She saw potential. And she believed that, with the right education, Black girls could change not only their own lives but the world. For her, these young Black women were worth every public request, every pleading letter, every direct ask. Her love for them was so profound that it overshadowed her pride—she would go to any length to give them the chance they deserved.

Mary was also a strategist. She knew that the financial gap between Black and white communities was too vast to close on Black dollars alone. So she sought out white donors without a hint of shame or contradiction. To her, it wasn't about dependency; it was about being resourceful and doing what needed to be done for her girls.

Even the location of her school was a stroke of shrewd planning. Mary chose Daytona because it was underserved, with no public schools for Black children in sight, and because it was a winter haven for ultrawealthy white northerners. Every year, these "snowbirds" would escape the harsh New York, Connecticut, or Illinois winters, and arrive in Daytona—relaxed, open-hearted, and more jovial about the opportunity to do something good along the way. Mary knew how to position her school as a refreshing, worthy cause, one that just might capture their attention during their holiday stay. It worked like a charm.

Relationships matter. And Mary was masterful at building them. She prioritized connections with the class of liberal-minded out-of-town white folks who might be more open to supporting her school's mission. This support strategy that relied on the strength of weak ties was key to her school's survival.[1] Mary had a warmth and confidence that made others want to help; she wasn't just asking for favors—she was inspiring people to invest in the future of Black girls. Known for her famous sweet potato pies, she'd bring them to the Palmetto Club, a country club for winter visitors, using every opportunity to make herself known, make a connection, and make a case for her school. She'd bring her choir to perform at events, bringing her school's spirit and vision directly to the people she wanted to reach. Whether through fundraisers or casual meet-and-greets, Mary engaged both white and Black communities to support her vision, and for her, every contribution mattered—money, quilts, clothes, food. It was all fuel for the fire she was trying to light.

One of Mary's most remarkable gifts was her ability to foster a spirit of giving that crossed racial and class lines. People saw themselves in the Daytona Institute, and that was largely due to Mary's grace, her warmth, and her way of making people feel like they were a part of something bigger. She spent countless hours on the road, traveling to New York; Washington, DC; and beyond, meeting with politicians and business leaders—anyone who might lend support to her cause. Instead of simply asking for handouts, she was inviting people to be part of her vision.

Over time, her relentless charm and determination convinced some of the wealthiest white visitors who wintered in Daytona—people like John Rockefeller, James Gamble, and Samuel White—to join her school's board of trustees. This put her in proximity to an elite class of American society that few leaders of her time—white or Black—had access to.[2] Mary built close friendships with powerful women, including Eleanor Roosevelt, who visited her school multiple times. Through Eleanor, Mary also connected with President Franklin D. Roosevelt, who gifted her one of his canes, a nod to her signature style. In her beautiful dresses, fur coats, and with her Roosevelt cane in hand, Mary McLeod Bethune was a striking figure of Black excellence and leadership.

Behind this outward image of success and "Black girl magic" in succeeding to establish powerful alliances, her reality on the ground was infuriating. Despite having some of the richest, most powerful people in the world in her corner, people who genuinely respected her, who admired her mission, and who supported her—the financial footing of her school was always on shaky ground. None of them ever gave enough to fully endow her school or to give her the security and peace of mind that a single large donation could have offered. Now, I'm not saying they owed her anything. But at the time, it was customary for major white institutions that had boards stacked with influential supporters to receive large gifts that guaranteed their futures. Those institutions didn't have to worry about next month's bills; they could focus on growth, on the future, on carrying out a bold, long-term vision. Black schools, meanwhile, were left in a constant state of financial precarity, with Black leaders like Mary scrambling and scraping to survive. This was the cruel reality for Mary and for so many Black educators running private schools during Jim Crow: surrounded by wealth and influence, yet constantly forced to fight just to keep the doors open.[3] For Mary and many others, the wealthy, white, and powerful were only willing to go so far.

The hypocrisy of white philanthropy during this time is glaring. If they believed in these Black institutions so deeply, if they truly saw the potential in these schools, then why didn't they fully fund them? White schools were endowed, given enough to ensure their longevity and success. Presidents and administrators at these institutions didn't spend sleepless nights wondering whether they'd have to shut down or whether they'd be able to keep the lights on another year. They were free to focus solely on their educational missions because the support was there, solid and unshakable. But for Black schools, even the most exceptional ones like Bethune's Daytona Institute, that level of commitment was nearly nonexistent.

Though there was some support. Andrew Carnegie personally contributed to Bethune's efforts to establish a Black nursing school and hospital on her campus. This filled a pressing need during the Jim Crow era. Black people were turned from white hospitals and had virtually no opportunities to train as nurses or doctors in white medical schools. Bethune recognized the urgent need for Black health care facilities and training programs, so she made it happen. She was able to do it because she had seen it before. Lucy Craft Laney had paved the way by founding the first Black nursing school in Georgia at the Haines. Laney's institution trained generation after generation of Black nurses who had nowhere else to go for education. In this way, Black private schools were lifelines to their communities. They filled voids intentionally created by a country that chose, again and again, to shut Black people out.

★ ★ ★

Mary, Charlotte, Lucy, and their peers didn't have the luxury of time or endless resources. Black children needed education immediately—there was no waiting, no gradual buildup. That's why these schools grew at breakneck speeds. Lucy Craft Laney started with five students, and within a year, she was teaching over two hundred. Bethune's Daytona Institute followed the same explosive growth pattern. The need was real, and these women felt the crushing weight of that responsibility. Yet they were often criticized by their donors for expanding "too fast." But those criticisms came from people who would never know what it was like.

Imagine being one of these Black women educators, standing at your door and seeing mothers and fathers pleading with you to take in their child, to open just one more spot, knowing full well that your resources are stretched to their breaking point. These women carried that weight on their shoulders every single day. They took on more than seemed reasonable or possible—not out of arrogance or ambition but out of a deep, almost desperate sense of duty. They understood that if they didn't step up, those children would have nowhere else to go. They knew that turning a child away was often a sentence.

Black women educators made miracles happen, not because they wanted glory but because they understood that the survival and dignity of their communities depended on their schools.

★ ★ ★

Charlotte Hawkins Brown's journey wasn't free from the overbearing weight of white philanthropy either. She began her career as a school founder under the shadow of abandonment. The American Missionary Association (AMA), which initially backed her, pulled its support and left her scrambling to piece together funding for what would become Palmer Institute. Determined to make it work, Charlotte returned to Massachusetts, calling on every connection she had. She spoke at churches, both Black and white, accepting whatever small donations she could pull together. Alice Freeman Palmer, her mentor and anchor, was her most powerful ally, opening doors and connecting Charlotte to wealthy New Englanders who saw in her the potential to "uplift the race."

When Palmer died suddenly, Charlotte lost a personal mentor and a crucial link in her network. But she turned the loss into strategy, persuading the Palmer family to let her name the school in her mentor's honor. Her choice to name it Palmer Memorial Institute was a stamp of legitimacy that Charlotte knew would open even more doors. At just nineteen, Charlotte Hawkins Brown was pulling off feats that seasoned fundraisers would envy, juggling emotion, strategy, and the urgent needs of her community to make her school a reality.

Yet from the beginning, her donors' gifts came with a price, where every dollar held strings, conditions, and condescension. One of her earliest benefactors, Mary R. Grinnell, was generous with her financial support for Palmer's industrial programs. But Grinnell wasn't content to just give; she wanted to tell Charlotte what to do. She regularly imposed her "advice" on Charlotte, outlining how to run Palmer, shaping its curriculum, and reinforcing her own paternalistic vision of what a Black school should be. Charlotte, who was as proud as she was pragmatic, had to grit her teeth and nod along, knowing that this was what it took to keep the funds flowing.

Another donor, Helen Kimball, gave two hundred acres of land, a generous gift with a patronizing twist—she insisted that seventy of those acres be dedicated to "practical agriculture" to support the school's food needs. It was a classic move: support that reinforced industrial education that so many white philanthropists promoted. And the demands didn't stop there. Frances Guthrie, yet another benefactor, had the nerve to send Charlotte a twenty-six-page document instructing her on how to manage Palmer's curriculum, peppered with warnings not to "teach her pupils more than their natures could receive."[4]

Imagine the daily exhaustion of managing these demands—the constant patronizing letters, the stipulations hidden in every gift, the balancing act Charlotte performed to appease these donors without betraying her vision. This was the tightrope she walked: keeping her school's doors open while swallowing her pride, navigating a world where even support came with a heavy dose of disrespect. And through it all, she pushed forward, proving that her commitment to Palmer, to her students, and to the future of Black education was stronger than any chain these donors tried to clench around her.

Charlotte Hawkins Brown was an expert at nurturing relationships with northern donors. She knew how to charm them, inspire them, and make them feel invested in her mission. And yet, even with all these connections, the financial reality was relentless. Most gifts she received, even when they amounted to $800 or $2,000—respectable sums at the time—were only enough to keep Palmer Institute barely afloat. Charlotte lived in a constant state of fundraising triage, chasing the next donation just to cover the next expense.

Then, in 1910, a breakthrough came. Galen L. Stone, a white Boston philanthropist, became her most important backer. Stone was different from the others. He didn't confine his support to the typical industrial model that most white donors favored for Black education. Instead, he asked her directly, "What do you want to do?" For the first time, Charlotte felt a donor's genuine trust in her vision for the school. This freedom allowed her to break away from the confines of the industrial education model and pursue higher academic and cultural aspirations, crafting a curriculum that aligned with her dreams, not just her donors' expectations.

Stone's support was transformative. It gave Charlotte the breathing room she needed to focus on producing informed, cultured citizens who could navigate and challenge the world they were entering. His financial support was a game changer, but so was the confidence he showed in her leadership. It was at this turning point that she shifted her school into the finishing school it is remembered as today.

Through sheer persistence, Charlotte even managed to reach Charles Eliot, the president of Harvard University. Eliot lent his name to her cause, a powerful endorsement that gave her institution a new level of prestige and opened doors to more fundraising channels. But even the endorsement of Harvard's president couldn't translate into the kind of substantial, no-strings-attached support that white institutions enjoyed. Eliot's name looked good on paper, but it didn't erase the realities of her financial precarity. This was the bittersweet irony of Charlotte's world: she had proximity to power, she could call on the president of Harvard, yet she still struggled to secure the resources she needed. It was a glaring reminder of the limits of Black–white solidarities in the battle for the Black mind— an endorsement, a handshake, or a pat on the back couldn't replace real, lasting financial support.

But the demands on Charlotte never let up. There were fires— literal ones that destroyed buildings on campus and figurative ones as she scrambled to appease donors, cover bills, and fight off the ever-present threat of closure. Like other Black school founders, Charlotte spent more and more time on the road than at her school, constantly chasing donations to keep Palmer alive. This relentless travel was a grueling sacrifice that wore her down and took a toll on her health and her spirit. Yet, it was a burden she carried nearly all her life. Failure was never an option, no matter the personal cost.

Both Mary McLeod Bethune and Charlotte Hawkins Brown built lasting Black institutions, brick by painstaking brick. Forming boards of trustees that included wealthy white elites was no small feat; it was a strategic move that added legitimacy, attracted donations, and kept their schools alive. They knew that having the right kind people on board could open doors, even if those same people sometimes shut them out in other ways. But these women's success didn't just come from seeking support from white people. They built alliances with other women, both Black and white, to amplify their cause.

White women, especially those from the upper crust of society, often became indispensable allies, helping raise funds and sometimes leveraging their husbands' wealth and influence. These alliances, complicated as they were, created a multiracial support network essential to the survival of their schools.

Lucy Craft Laney, Mary McLeod Bethune, and Charlotte Hawkins Brown were not just educators in the traditional sense. They were founders—business strategists and visionaries who harnessed every tool available to them. They ran businesses in an era when even their need to exist was questioned. The fact that they bought land, founded institutions, shaped curricula, hired faculty, and marketed their schools to both local and national audiences—all in the face of Jim Crow—is nothing short of incredible.

Think about what these women achieved. They were moguls of Black education, wielding business acumen, marketing genius, and sheer vision. In another time, we might celebrate them with the same fervor we reserve for "tech bros" and Silicon Valley start-up founders. They were entrepreneurs in the truest sense, redefining what it meant to be a Black educator.

So let these women inspire you. Pause, reflect on all they did. What their legacies remind us is that real power lies in vision, strategy, and an unbreakable commitment to our communities.

CHAPTER 7

Millionaire Monarchs

Imagine you went outside and planted a seed for a tree. Would you expect it to grow overnight? Would you stand over it the next day, tapping your foot, wondering, *When are you going to grow?* Of course not. You'd understand that growth takes time, patience, and nurturing. You'd have a vision for how the tree might one day reshape the landscape of where you planted it—creating some shade, penetrating its roots into the soil, taking up space, and influencing the environment around it. That's exactly how those behind the Tuskegee Machine approached Black education. They were playing the long game.

They weren't just growing a tree; they were planting a whole forest with each institution, each school, each dollar, and each leader they positioned to reflect their vision for Black futures.

The story of the rise of the Tuskegee Machine is a story about power—the kind that moves slowly and quietly but leaves enduring marks. This was power that worked its way into institutions, into textbooks, and into the minds of children and teachers alike. This elusive cabal didn't exert control overtly. Instead, they invested in long-term strategies they hoped would shape Black education in ways that reflected their own values and agendas. By the time Black leaders caught on, the roots of this educational philosophy had already dug deep into the soil, setting up a system that was difficult to resist, let alone uproot.

Starting in the 1880s, after Reconstruction's promise of democracy came crashing down, a cabal of educators, business leaders, and philanthropists banded together with a singular aim: to control Black education in ways that would keep Black people in certain roles at the bottom rungs of society. These influential figures carefully sowed the seeds of their educational philosophy, insisting that industrial education was the only path forward for Black Americans—a path that trained them in trades and manual skills but left little room for academic or intellectual growth. They called it practical. They called it realistic. But in reality, their actions were about placing a ceiling on what Black people could dream for themselves.

This was the Tuskegee Machine—a multidecade playbook written behind closed doors, where all players knew their part. And by the time this network of power-solidified, independent Black school founders like Lucy Craft Laney, Mary McLeod Bethune, and Charlotte Hawkins Brown were left scrambling for scraps, raising funds from church collection plates and community bake sales, all the while the Tuskegee Machine was making it rain from the seats of corporate boardrooms.

The founders of the Tuskegee Machine invested in a long-term vision that they promoted at conferences and by funneling money into Black schools that followed their blueprint, spreading literature, serving on boards, and by wielding their power behind the scenes to ensure that their vision for Black education became a reality.

A little over twenty years into their endeavor, in the early 1900s, what started as small, scattered efforts had grown into a full-fledged industry of Black education. A tsunami of new money flooded into the southern educational system, with the lion's share of the money committed to Black education under the Hampton-Tuskegee reach. What had started out as a patchwork experiment evolved into a full-fledged ecosystem, a global one at that.

The Slater Fund, with its $1 million investment, planted the initial seed of large-scale philanthropy in Black education in America. But that was little money compared to what was to come. A new wave of ultrawealthy philanthropists stepped on the scene pouring over one hundred times more dollars into their pet projects than their predecessor. While not all funds went directly into Black education, the portion that did was enough to transform the entire field.

Between 1901 and 1913, this new breed of philanthropy was exemplified by giants like the Rockefeller Foundation and the Carnegie Corporation. Armed with endowments of $100 million and $135 million, respectively, these organizations transformed America's social safety net by infusing it with unprecedented capital.[1] The Rockefeller Foundation played a significant role in eradicating hookworm in the American South, addressing a widespread public health issue that had debilitated countless communities. This achievement alone demonstrates how big philanthropy, with its agility and resources, can tackle urgent societal issues more swiftly than government agencies burdened by bureaucracy. But with this power came a double-edged sword. These big philanthropies, left unchecked, also used their vast sums of money to power a machine that attempted to subjugate Black education just as it was taking root.

These juggernauts weren't the only players on the field, though. Smaller but equally impactful foundations, like the General Education Board (GEB) and the Southern Education Board, alongside specific Rockefeller creations like the Laura Spelman Rockefeller

Foundation, all targeted Black education in the South. They were joined by others like the Jeanes Fund, the Rosenwald Fund, and the Phelps-Stokes Fund—all of which shared in the goal of shaping the educational future of Black America. Collectively, they were instrumental in directing the course of education, investing heavily in industrial and vocational models that echoed the Hampton-Tuskegee framework and advancing an agenda that would define education for Black Americans throughout the early twentieth century.[2]

By this time, philanthropy wasn't just about handing out money; it was about wielding influence over educational policy.

This group of philanthropies didn't work in isolation. Think of them like the cartoon *The Transformers*. Each organization operated individually, but when they aligned, they became a powerful Voltron, pushing their Tuskegee Machine agenda forward with even more force. Instead of competing with one another they aligned their interests and resources, and they kept control by serving on one another's boards.

Booker T. Washington's star ascended during this era. He operated like a politician backed by wealthy corporate donors, moving with the quiet expectation that he would do their bidding. Washington and the Tuskegee Institute benefited tremendously from aligning with these philanthropic donors. But his role was pivotal. They needed him not just as a figurehead but as the Black spokesperson of the Hampton-Tuskegee model, pushing their educational vision forward on a global scale.

Washington's involvement shows just how layered and complex the power structures within the Tuskegee Machine really were. Everyone had a role to play—from the philanthropists pulling the purse strings to Black leaders like Washington, who became the voice and symbol of their agenda. This wasn't about white power simply dictating everything; rather, it was about a nuanced interplay between Black and white interests. Washington's public image provided legitimacy and influence that transcended both Black and white audiences, showing that power is rarely exerted by a sledgehammer.

We're seeing striking parallels today with initiatives like Project 2025, a meticulously crafted playbook backed by some of our countries most influential conservative think tanks and politicians. Much like the Tuskegee Machine, Project 2025 isn't just about a single policy or a short-term political win. It's a long game. If successful, this project plans to reshape policies and key government positions under our current right-wing conservative administration. Among its most alarming goals? Defunding agencies that support equity and justice, and even shutting down the Department of Education. If their seeds of power and control are allowed to grow, it won't matter who's in office or what voters want; the agenda would be set in stone, leaving little room for change. This isn't just a plan for policy change—it's a form of state capture. The Tuskegee Machine understood then, as right-wing conservatives do now, that long-term control isn't about visible power; it's about the quiet ability to shape institutions and public opinion over generations.

That's how the Tuskegee Machine operated in its attempt to control Black education. Leaders didn't just want to influence one or two schools; they aimed for a complete takeover—controlling the curriculum, the staff, the research, the entire educational agenda. Their long game was to ensure that their vision of Black education outlived them, stretching across generations.

And, sure, you might be thinking, *Well, wasn't the money a good thing? Didn't Black communities need that kind of investment?* And in a sense, you'd be right. With southern states still refusing to adequately fund Black public schools, these donations were a lifeline for many Black institutions.

But it's not so different from imagining today's tech billionaires—Elon Musk, Bill Gates, Jeff Bezos—suddenly offering to pour millions into underserved Black communities for educational initiatives. Would you trust their intentions completely, or would you raise an eyebrow and keep your guard up?

That was the position Black communities found themselves in back then. Significant financial investments from philanthropic foundations were a double-edged sword. By the early 1900s, the Tuskegee Machine reached its peak. It had grown into a decentralized yet formidable force backed by staggering wealth and influence. I'm going to show you how the masterminds behind the Tuskegee Machine moved and how they strategically propped up Booker T. Washington in power. But first, let me take you back to where it all began, to the story of how the millionaire monarchs "discovered" Black education in the South—all starting with a little train ride with a friend.

Robert C. Ogden was the pied piper of the Hampton-Tuskegee model. He had a knack for luring America's wealthiest men to the southern Black belt.

The Philadelphia tycoon amassed his fortune in the late 1800s, through a lucrative partnership with Wanamaker's, one of America's first department stores. However, Ogden's true passion was clear: he believed that the South's economic survival—and by extension, America's progress—depended on solving the "Negro problem" through education. He knew words alone wouldn't be convincing enough. He needed to show his rich friends what the Hampton-Tuskegee model of education could do.

He hosted annual all-expenses paid group tours through the South. Sparing no expense, he would rent out an entire train from the Pennsylvania Railroad Company so he could wine and dine his guests in luxury as they traveled from New York to Alabama. It was on these lavish "Ogden train" excursions where America's business elite were courted, introduced to the Hampton-Tuskegee idea, and persuaded to join the movement.[3]

One notable train rider was a twenty-six-year-old John D. Rockefeller Jr. Fresh out of Brown University, where he had earned his bachelor's degree, Rockefeller had just joined the family business. Like his parents, his interests stretched far beyond oil and profits. He was already deeply curious about how the family's wealth could be used to shape society. His father had made several modest donations to Black schools in the South, including gifting the land where Morehouse College stands today. Likewise, his mother, Laura Spelman Rockefeller, had supported Black women's education since the 1880s, notably becoming the namesake of Spelman College. However, despite these acts of generosity, the Rockefellers had not yet formalized their giving strategy. That was about to change.

Ogden's invitation came at a time when he was hungry for a cause that aligned with his burgeoning sense of mission. The sight of rural poverty was a reality check for Rockefeller. On the tour, he witnessed firsthand the dilapidated homes, the decaying plantations, and the pervasive poverty that plagued both Black and white southerners. This was no Manhattan, with its booming economy and grand architecture. Instead, Rockefeller was confronted with disease-ridden communities, high rates of illiteracy, and an entrenched racial hatred that threatened any vision of a prosperous and unified America. For him, these sights were a call to action.

Upon his return to New York, young Rockefeller sat down with his father, John D. Rockefeller Sr., and the two made a commitment—$1 million to establish a new philanthropy, the GEB. Rockefeller Sr.'s commitment to the GEB didn't stop there. Just four years into its operation, he increased his contributions to a staggering $43 million. Over the board's lifetime, from 1903 to 1964, the GEB would go on to spend $60 million—about 18 percent of its total funds—on Black education in the South, making an enormous impact on educational opportunities in the region.[4] This monumental financial commitment not only demonstrated the Rockefellers' philanthropic power but also illustrated the critical role that private funding played in shaping the landscape of education for African Americans during a time when state and federal support was scarce. However, in-line with the Tuskegee Machine strategy, the GEB set its focus on incentivizing state and local school boards to provide matching funds to support creating Black public elementary schools teaching industrial education.

The powerful white men behind the scenes set the larger agenda. Booker T. Washington's role was to sell it.

By 1900, Washington spent most of his time crisscrossing the country, delivering speeches in New York and Boston, and playing his part in the grand strategy orchestrated by the trustees. These men controlled the fundraising events, bringing in the "Who's Who" of Manhattan society. They needed Washington to present a vision of Black uplift that was palatable to wealthy, white audiences. His story as a former slave who'd risen to lead an institution resonated deeply, but it was his message of self-help, thrift, and gradual acceptance—devoid of any real critique of white supremacy—that sealed the deal. He didn't dwell on Jim Crow's brutal realities or the gross underfunding of Black schools. Instead, Washington assured white benefactors that, with their support, Black people would quietly lift themselves up by their bootstraps, without agitating for political or social equality.

One such benefactor was Andrew Carnegie, the steel magnate whose fortune at the time was an astronomical $350 million (about $6.5 billion today). Carnegie first encountered Washington's charm in 1899, after hearing him speak at Madison Square Garden. Impressed by Washington's presentation and perhaps more by the white power structure backing him, Carnegie began making annual $10,000 donations to Tuskegee. Then in 1903, Carnegie made an unprecedented move: he donated $600,000 to Tuskegee's endowment, a story that got the attention of the *New York Times*. What really caught the media's attention, though, was the provision that guaranteed Booker T. Washington and his wife a lifetime income—a financial cushion unheard of for Black leaders at the time. Tuskegee and GEB trustee William H. Baldwin praised Washington in the press as "the modern Moses," leading Black people "to the land of milk and honey."[5]

Washington earned wealth and influence from his position, while his fellow members of the Tuskegee Machine gained the symbolic advantage of having a Black figurehead. It was a partnership built on mutual benefit, but the balance of power was clear: Washington may have been the charismatic face of the movement, but behind him, it was the Machine calling the shots.

As northern capital flowed into southern education, Hampton Institute and Tuskegee Institute became the prototypes for how Black education should look. Washington's work provided the proof of concept, attracting ever-larger sums to expand the Machine's influence. These weren't just schools anymore—they were institutional models designed to train Black people to exist within a white supremacist system, attracting praise and funding from those who stood to benefit from keeping that system intact. At this point, the world was watching.

In 1901, the German government initiated a collaboration with the Machine to establish Tuskegee-inspired schools in Togo, a German colony in West Africa at the time. The aim was to implement industrial education, believing that African American educators could "civilize" the African population. The idea was to transplant Tuskegee's industrial education approach to Africa, where African Americans could teach agricultural methods to local Togolese communities so they could labor in cotton fields Germany had established on Togolese land.[6]

This project unfolded during the "scramble for Africa," a period of aggressive European colonization. In 1870, European powers controlled only 10 percent of Africa. By 1914, Europe had brutally colonized 90 percent of the continent. The exploitation of African land and resources, driven by industrialization and competition among European empires, created an opening for educational models like Tuskegee's to be exported to Africa. Washington's involvement, in partnership with his trustees, was part of this larger context, wherein Europe began to take a serious interest in the US southern educational models that aligned with their imperial ambitions.

However, the experiment in Togo was not a success. It quickly became clear that the challenges of applying the Tuskegee model in a colonial African context were far more complicated than anticipated. The partnership between Tuskegee and German colonial authorities proved problematic due to cultural, political, and logistical barriers, and the project eventually collapsed.

Though the Togo project failed, it marked the beginning of broader ambitions, setting the stage for future international experiments.

European colonizers weren't the only ones with their eyes on Tuskegee. Across the African diaspora, Black leaders, educators, and visionaries found something compelling in what the school, and its leader, represented. From afar, Tuskegee symbolized a form of Black self-determination that felt revolutionary—an institution run by Black leaders, for Black minds. For those abroad who had been shut out of formal education entirely, Tuskegee was a lighthouse guiding the path to liberation. Figures like John Dube, who was determined to build something similar for his people in South Africa, saw in Tuskegee the inspiration for Black South Africans to create their own institutions and uplift their communities.

Dube was among the four hundred Black South Africans who came to America seeking educational opportunity at the turn of the twentieth century. When he set shores for the US, no schools existed for Black South Africans, leaving them in a similar position as African Americans were at the end of the Civil War.[7]

During one of his visits, in 1897, Dube witnessed Booker T. Washington deliver a speech at a Black church in Brooklyn. What he witnessed left an indelible mark on his soul. Here was this Black man commanding the attention of a large audience, preaching the power of Black self-help, thrift, land ownership, and education. For Dube, Washington's message resonated as a call to action to create something similar for his own people. He did not dwell on the limitations of the Tuskegee model—he saw in it a blueprint for progress and self-sufficiency that he could bring home.

With this inspiration, Dube returned home to establish the Zulu Christian Industrial Institute on land donated by his family, opening its doors in 1900 as the first Black-led school in South Africa. Dube's school was built by Black hands and aimed to teach Black minds. This was a revolutionary act in a society so fiercely committed to Black subjugation. Dube's role as an educational free-dom fighter eventually fed into a larger movement for political lib-eration. Shortly after he opened his school, he was appointed as the first president of the African National Congress—the political party later led by Nelson Mandela that took down South Africa's Apartheid regime.[8]

Globalization, Black international migration, and colonization by the British, French, German, Belgian, and Dutch empires gave birth to a new kind of Black cosmopolitanism and political thought. Dube's mission is but one example of how Black leaders across the globe saw what they needed in the Tuskegee model—a path to independence and uplift. For some, Tuskegee represented the possi-bilities of Black autonomy and institutional power, sparking change that would reverberate far beyond America's borders. Others, on the other hand, saw it as a powerful tool of control and subjugation.

"Ladies and gentlemen," he began, his confident voice slicing through the quiet air. Clutching his notes, the keynote speaker stood tall before the esteemed Philosophical Institute of Edinburgh, in his childhood homeland of Scotland. "So many and varied have been the subjects treated by my predecessors in your long history, that one has some dif-ficulty in selecting a theme." His presence alone was enough to com-mand attention, but now he was about to veer from Europe's most pressing issues. Instead, this titan of industry had his sights set on a problem an ocean away, in a land not of his birth but one tied to his fortune. "I escape this," he continued, "by breaking fresh ground in bringing to your attention: The Negro in America."[9]

Andrew Carnegie—a figure equally revered and resented—stood no taller than his words, but the power behind them was mighty. With his neatly trimmed beard and measured cadence, he leaned into the podium, fully aware of the weight of his message. The world's elite had gathered to hear him, a man with the rare distinction of being both one of the wealthiest individuals on the planet and one of its most enthusiastic philanthropists. His topic, "The Negro in America," placed the so-called problem of Black Americans on a global stage, emphasizing its importance among Europe's ruling class. "No racial movement in the world today is more interesting; few, if any, are more important," Carnegie asserted, and the grand hall fell silent.

This wasn't a spontaneous concern for Carnegie; it had been building in the backdrop of global geopolitics. The scramble for Africa was almost complete by the time he took the podium in 1907. The violent race for dominance had sparked white anxiety over what to do with their new Black subjects, many of whom vastly outnumbered their colonizers. For Europeans, Africa was an untamed, resource-rich territory, and its people were the inconvenient truth that came with the spoils. Meanwhile, the United States, having long since "conquered" its Black population through centuries of slavery, had unwittingly become a case study for European powers. What Carnegie's speech revealed, beneath the veneer of philanthropy, was the interest in applying the politics of American racial domination as a model for colonial rule. And Black America was at the center of that conversation.

From there, Carnegie dove into an account of the progress Black Americans had made since Emancipation. He rattled off facts like a dutiful historian: "In 1865, the Negroes were without homes of their own. In 1900, thirty-five years later, there were 372,414 owners of homes, and of these 225,156 were free of encumbrance." Such statistics painted a neat picture of the American Dream at work, ignoring the vicious structural barriers that made such accomplishments miracles in themselves. To Carnegie, Black progress—specifically through homeownership—served as a bulwark against "revolutionary or socialistic ideas." Order, after all, was paramount.

But Carnegie wasn't done. He offered stern criticisms, voicing what many white elites believed but didn't always say outright: the United States had given too much too soon. In his view, full citizenship and political rights, including the right to vote, were premature for African Americans. And liberal education? Carnegie had choice words for that too, describing it as "moral dynamite" capable of inciting rebellion. He likened such teaching to giving "subject races" a "deadly explosive" that could someday tear down those who taught it. It was a peculiar admission—an understanding that education could either liberate or subjugate, depending on who controlled it.

The crowd sat in silence, no doubt absorbing both the message and the man behind it. Then Carnegie addressed the issue that many Americans—including himself—could not ignore: lynching. His take was as convenient as it was cruel. He acknowledged the racial violence but downplayed its frequency, blaming the victims for being guilty of crimes. "Judge Lynch," he said, "is rarely, if ever, accused of punishing the innocent."

Still, Carnegie's speech wasn't entirely grim. He ended with a hopeful, if naive, vision of the future: a peaceful coexistence between Black and white Americans, one that was profitable for both races. It was a vision built on a house of cards.

What the audience in Edinburgh didn't know was that just a year prior, Carnegie had visited Tuskegee Institute for the first time, three years after his unprecedented $600,000 donation to the school. What he saw far exceeded his expectations. The order, the cleanliness, the students eagerly toiling away—it confirmed everything he wanted to believe.

As he closed his speech, Carnegie stood by his beliefs in gradual, controlled advancement through industrial education. His vision for Black Americans was one of quiet progress, not equity. And though Carnegie likely left the stage feeling optimistic, what was set in motion by men like him would soon begin to unravel. The Tuskegee idea, for all its financial backing, could only go so far before the fault lines began to show.

And as for those colonial bridges being built between the Tuskegee Machine and Europe? Their influence would soon be felt, in a big way, in the Motherland.

I've been going back and forth to South Africa for over twenty years now, but things really intensified for me in 2016 when I began going out there regularly for research, which eventually led to me becoming a Fulbright Fellow. The time I've spent there has always been charged with a sense of urgency. I was there researching the complexities of Black education so that I could get some of the material I needed to write this book. But something changed when I got there in 2016. That's when the *#RhodesMustFall* and *#FeesMustFall* movements were underway—at the University of Cape Town and Witwatersrand University—sparking global uproar. The movements swept through universities in South Africa, down to Zimbabwe, across the ocean to Europe, and all the way over to the United States, hitting the shores of Ivy League campuses like Harvard Law School.

These movements were about exposing the colonial roots of institutions that Black people—particularly in South Africa—were still struggling to access. Institutions that continue to lock Black people out of economic prosperity and keep them on the fringes, even today. According to the World Bank, South Africa is *the* most unequal country in the world, where the top 10 percent of the population—comprised of almost all-white South Africans—holds more than 80 percent of the wealth and land.[10] This inequity is deeply rooted in the nation's history of Apartheid and colonialism, which systematically marginalized Black South Africans. And these legacies of exclusion still loom large today. For instance, while Black South Africans represent 80 percent of the population, they comprise less than 20 percent of college students. Disparities like these simply put deep-seated racial inequities on autopilot. Black South Africans often have less access to quality education due to high fees and double-digit tuition hikes, which in turn limits their opportunities for higher-paying jobs and contributes to the persistent wealth gap. That's why the "*Fall*-ist" movements were just as much material as they were visceral.

On March 9, 2015, Chumani Maxwele, an undergrad student at the University of Cape Town, hurled a bucket of shit onto a monument of Cecil John Rhodes. Yes—his own boo boo. And when you looked at that statue, grand and regal, perched right there on top of that hill, surveying what he considered "his" land—the connections are clear. Rhodes was a man who built his fortune off brutal colonialism, and his likeness was sitting in the middle of a campus that Black South Africans were still fighting to have a sliver of access to. Maxwele's protest didn't just spark outrage—it sparked a global movement. One that spread to Zimbabwe, the UK, and eventually to us in the US, with Royall Must Fall at Harvard.

Three years later, on April 30, 2018, Maya Little took it even further. This PhD student at University of North Carolina Chapel Hill mixed red paint with her own blood and threw it onto the Silent Sam monument, which had been looming over the campus entrance since 1913. That statue of a Confederate soldier—a monument praising the fight to maintain slavery—was a symbol of white supremacy, standing tall on the campus of one of this country's most prestigious state universities. After decades of letter-writing campaigns, protests, and demands to take that thing down, Maya Little's spontaneous act of protest became the tipping point. After much back and forth with the university and the police, that same semester, students literally tore the statue down with their bare hands.

Here's why this matters in our discussion about dead white men: these figures weren't just statues. They were symbols of the exclusion, hostility, and invisibility that Black and Indigenous students still face at these institutions. They were reminders of the legacies of exclusion and exploitation that still impact Black student life today. Centuries of slavery, Jim Crow, colonialism, extraction, and exclusion don't just disappear—they leave scars. These student-led movements were about more than taking down monuments—they were about decolonizing the entire education system. It's about restructuring who gets to tell the story. Who gets to have a seat at the table. It's about *finally* letting those who've been historically shut out not only get in, but belong and thrive.

These movements are part of a much larger collapse of history happening in real time. The histories and fates of Black folks across the globe are linked—what happens in Africa affects us here, and vice versa. Or as William Monroe Trotter so sharply put it in his newspaper: "None of us are free till all of us are free."

So when those students marched with banners proclaiming, "All Rhodes lead to colonization," they were cutting right to the core of it. This isn't just about the past—it's about the legacy of people like Rhodes and what they left behind. That is why we must examine the story of Cecil Rhodes and what his fortune did to understand why this fight continues today.

★ ★ ★

After graduating with a bachelor's degree from Oxford University, Cecil John Rhodes set sail for the Cape Colony in 1881 in search of his life's purpose. He found it in business and politics. He was a man consumed by ambition, intent on shaping the world to his liking. His life's work was marked by a relentless pursuit of control and domination. In his relatively short lifetime, Rhodes managed to colonize a vast stretch of southern Africa, so much so that he audaciously named an entire country after himself—Rhodesia, now modern-day Zambia and Zimbabwe.

Southern Africa boasts a bounty of mineral resources, and Rhodes made it his business to extract them. He founded the Gold Fields of South Africa Company in 1885 and three years later, in 1888, the De Beers Consolidated Mines. In less than a decade, by 1891, his companies were responsible for mining 90 percent of the world's diamond supply. And De Beers still controls that supply today.

Through his industrial mining enterprise, Rhodes became one of the wealthiest people on earth during his lifetime. However, for him, his fortune was simply a financial means to a political end: the creation of a new world order ruled by what he called "the Anglo-Saxon race."

However, fate would not allow him to see his dream fully actualized. At the age of forty-eight, Rhodes succumbed to the heart failure that had plagued him for most of his life. In his short lifetime, he did, however, manage to colonize much of southern Africa, extracting her resources for profit and exploiting the lands and forcing hundreds of thousands of Black South Africans into dangerous, backbreaking work in the mines.

His name is etched in history for time immemorial—on the names of universities in South Africa and in England at his alma mater, Oxford. His name and image are on monuments, companies, and, for a time, entire countries. One of Rhodes's lasting contributions to this vision of global domination was the creation of the Rhodes Scholarship.

With his eye looking to the next two hundred years of empire building, he created an endowed trust for the Rhodes Scholars program in his last will and testament. He set up a scholarship to bring together the world's "young colonists"—men from the various colonies of the British empire, including the US, who would soon take the reins in ruling the world.[11] Sensing that his ideas would outlive him, Rhodes was meticulous about detailing his wishes for his fortune.

The scholarship was originally created for selected students to attend Oxford. The idea was to foster a sense of pride and shared vision among the future leaders of the Anglo empire. Rhodes had outlined territorial quotas for the scholarship, with specified territories in South Africa and Australia claiming three-quarters of what were termed the "colonial scholarships." Other regions included territories in the British West Indies, the Atlantic Islands, and parts of Canada. The lion's share of scholarships, however, were allocated to the United States. He appropriated two scholarships per state to the "American Scholarships," totaling fifty American Rhodes Scholars per year vis-à-vis twenty annual awards for all others.

Rhodes was clear in his will that he did not want the committee to select candidates who were "merely bookworms." Instead, he was looking for young men of promising character and physique, noting the importance of "success in manly outdoor sports," "instincts to lead," and "sympathy for the protection of the weak." Interestingly, the great colonist took special care to specify that "no student shall be qualified or disqualified for election to a scholarship on account of his race or religious opinions."

Incredibly, the first Black Rhodes Scholar, Alain Locke, slipped through the cracks in 1907. Locke went on to earn his PhD in philosophy at Harvard and then returned to teaching at the acclaimed HBCU Howard University. There, he trained a generation of Black minds to value and center Black history, art, and culture in all they did—from writing to art to teaching. Locke would go on to become one of the architects of the Harlem Renaissance.[12] Yet it would take another half century for another Black Rhodes Scholar to emerge.

Left on its own, this race-blind caveat may have suggested that Cecil Rhodes saw all subjects under the British Crown as potential equals. However, he instructed his executor to publish chapters on his writings and political beliefs alongside his will so that his wishes would be understood in context.[13]

"I contend that we are the first race in the world, and that the more of the world we inhabit the better it is for the human race," Rhodes penned in a letter attached to his will. "I contend that every acre added to our territory means the birth of more of the English race who otherwise would not be brought into existence." Rhodes developed his own philosophy that served as a North Star guiding all his actions, in life and after death. He believed in the superiority of English-speaking whites. He dreamed of forming a secret society of imperial citizens who would eventually bring all the people of the world under Anglo dominion.

Through this secret society, Rhodes shifted to envision a global federation of the English-speaking world. His goal was to bring the "whole uncivilized world" under the rule of the white English-speaking race. In his view, the Rhodes Scholars program would cultivate a new world identity for young colonists, pushing them to see themselves as a part of something much larger than any one country or territory. His greed for wealth and domination were boundless. Not even the heavens were safe. He remarked in his will: "To think of these stars that you see overhead at night, these vast worlds which we can never reach. I would annex the planets if I could; I often think of that. It makes me sad to see them so clear and yet so far."

The millionaire monarchs' investments created a robust infrastructure that could sustain their vision for generations. This infrastructure included prestigious scholarships like the Rhodes Scholars, research institutions funded by entities like the GEB, and numerous other mechanisms designed to perpetuate a controlled and hierarchical social order.

While the primary intent of these investments was to maintain control and reinforce existing power structures, the legacy of these efforts is complex. On one hand, they facilitated the creation of educational opportunities that were previously unimaginable for many African Americans and other marginalized groups. On the other hand, these opportunities were often structured in ways that reinforced subjugation and limited true social mobility. They embedded a system designed to control the masses while elevating a chosen few—that ensured the continuation of a world order rooted in white supremacy. The institutions and mechanisms they established continue to influence educational and social structures to this day, serving as both a testament to their vision and a reminder of the enduring complexities of education as a tool of power.

This was the new terrain that Black educators and school founders had to navigate. Oftentimes, they were unaware of how deep the Tuskegee Machine rabbit hole truly went.

CHAPTER 8

The Evil Genius

Let's look under the hood of the Tuskegee Machine and learn what was driving it forward. On one side stood the rise of big philanthropy, with its deep pockets and powerful connections, reinforcing the Tuskegee Machine with an armor of financial resources and political influence. On the other side was the social sciences—especially sociology—serving as the main weapon in its arsenal. Together, these forces were the engine driving the Tuskegee Machine's strategies and tactics in the battle for the Black mind, with long-lasting consequences for Black communities.

We live in a world that privileges science. Think about how often you hear phrases like "studies show," or how in everyday conversations we say, "prove it." Facts, data, and evidence have become the way we assert our points, advocate for ourselves, and legitimize our claims. But it wasn't always like this. This privileging of science over, say, one of Aristotle's philosophies or a religious doctrine is a relatively new way of thinking that took hold in the early 1900s—and that's no coincidence.

At the same time, the US was rapidly industrializing. And with that came an intense desire to rationalize everything. Industrial science was born, as companies tried to figure out how to squeeze the most productivity out of their workers. This is where we get the assembly line from—measuring productivity down to the second and predicting what changes could make businesses more efficient. These industrial ways of thinking also seeped into everyday life, putting social sciences on a pedestal as the most legitimate and respectable forms of knowledge—knowledge that was intended to secure people, resources, and power.

The world was changing fast, and sociology helped people make sense of it all. While Black people were still weighed down by the force of Jim Crow, excluded from most areas of national life, the rest of the country was moving on—getting more urban, more diverse, and wealthier. This was the era of massive immigration from Europe. Between 1900 and 1915, more than fifteen million European immigrants arrived in the United States—about as many as had come in the previous forty years combined. By 1910, three-quarters of New York City's population was either immigrants or first-generation Americans. These new Americans were primarily from southern and eastern Europe: Ireland, Poland, and Italy.

This wave of immigrants transformed the fabric of American life. Many settled in cities, taking jobs in booming industries like factories, railroads, and mining that powered the American economy. Immigration became key to fueling the nation's industrial machine.

While Black people were certainly making strides—earning degrees, starting businesses, organizing communities—there was an emerging Black middle class participating in these changes. But for the most part, Black people were legally barred from fully participating in this exciting time. Instead, Black life was largely confined to segregated spaces in the South. And inside these bubbles we created our own worlds, replete with vibrant traditions, cultures, and foodways that are still very much alive today.

So it's through research and data that government agencies and philanthropies determine who gets resources and how much. Social science became a tool of reason and justification—and that had significant consequences for Black education.

The first generation of Black sociologists emerged alongside the birth of American sociology. They, too, were trying to make sense of our world, and many focused on what they called "the race problem."

Black scholars like W. E. B. Du Bois were at the forefront. After earning his PhD from Harvard in 1894, he went on to produce the first empirical sociological study in the US in 1899: *The Philadelphia Negro*.[1] This was a landmark study for many reasons but especially because it challenged the prevailing beliefs about Black people. At the time, most white folks thought Black poverty, crime, and health issues were simply a reflection of Black people's "culture of poverty"—a kind of blame-the-victim mentality.

Du Bois's study turned that thinking upside down. He was commissioned by a group of wealthy white Philadelphians who assumed his study would confirm what they believed. Instead, what Du Bois revealed, using facts, data, and evidence, was that the Black residents in the city's Seventh Ward faced these challenges because they were excluded—from decent jobs, from living in good neighborhoods, from the full labor market. They were funneled into low-wage, unstable work, which led to high unemployment, poverty, and, ultimately, crime. His study used demographic data, interviews with families, maps—you name it. It was a full-scale sociological investigation.

Then there was Anna Julia Cooper, a scholar, educator, and fierce public speaker. In 1892, she published *A Voice from the South: By a Black Woman of the South.* This book was one of the first to shed light on the specific struggles Black women faced after Reconstruction. Cooper argued that Black women's education was essential to the progress of all Black people. Her book was one of the first to analyze the intersections of race and gender in the American South—what today we call intersectionality.[2]

Black sociologists like Du Bois and Cooper also worked hard to show the richness and diversity of Black life. And as we know, not all Black people were poor, uneducated, or the same in any way. Another Black sociologist, E. Franklin Frazier, highlighted the class diversity within the Black community through his research. He studied the Black middle class and showed how its members lived, how they built cultural institutions, and how their class status shaped their worldviews. His work was crucial in showing that Black life was dynamic, not static, and that we were a people on the move.[3]

These Blackademics and dozens of others took the focus off the tired old question "What's wrong with Black people?" and shifted it toward the real question: "What's wrong with the system?"

They weren't interested in treating symptoms. They were looking for the root causes of inequality. This is what we call "emancipatory sociology"—a sociology that not only diagnoses the problem but also offers solutions, pulling injustice up by its roots and dismantling systems that make life hard for some and easier for others.[4] They used sociology as a mighty weapon to attack oppressive systems at their core.

That's the foundation of Black sociology, and it's a legacy that runs deep in my veins. As a Black woman sociologist, my work isn't just academic—it's personal. I stand on the shoulders of giants like the ones mentioned above. Those who dared to use sociology as a tool for our liberation, not our oppression. My own scholarship delves into the historical roots of systemic racism, revealing the inner workings of how the structures that confine us today were built long before we were born. I've traced these systems from the institutionalization of the transatlantic slave trade in medieval times all the way to the seventeenth century to the African American Great Migration of the first half of the twentieth century. This book on racial inequality in education is about exposing the machinery that has kept us from our full potential and celebrating our rich Black educational tradition.

For me, this work is more than just history—it's a reckoning. I'm not interested in blaming individuals for the state of the world. Like the great Toni Morrison told us, "The very serious function of racism is a distraction. It keeps you from doing your work." Instead, I focus on the systems, the ideas, and the structures that shape our realities. I'm doing the kind of sociology that's meant to get us free, work that seeks to dismantle the very foundations of inequality. This is a continuation of the liberatory sociology that has been our mantle for over a century. Every piece of research, every lecture, every book is part of that larger fight to challenge injustice and advocate for equity.

But this path isn't without its shadows. Carrying this legacy as a Black woman, knowing the weight of the struggles that came before me, and pushing against forces that would rather maintain the status quo is not easy. But it's necessary.

Unfortunately, at the dawn of the twentieth century, sociology wasn't just a tool for progress. It was also weaponized to prop up racist ideologies. This was the height of what scholars refer to as "scientific racism." The Tuskegee Machine recognized sociology's power, and philanthropists began practicing what they called "scientific giving." This approach was based on studies and statistical findings rather than gut feelings. Gone were the days when philanthropic agents, men like Atticus Haygood, were able to persuade their trustees by saying "just trust me, bro."

Sociology opened the door to bigger funding streams, and it legitimized the work the Tuskegee Machine was doing. It allowed leaders to scale their efforts across the country.

It's one thing to make school-by-school recommendations for less or no funding, however, with the kind of arguments brought forth sociologically, one could make recommendations for an entire system. This shift made things less reliant on personalities like Booker T. Washington. Decisions could be made based on pseudoscience that pretended to be objective and neutral. Of course, it wasn't quite that simple, but that was the thinking.

And this brings us to the story of how the Tuskegee Machine recruited its newest all-star player. A sociologist named Thomas Jesse Jones—a man whom Du Bois dubbed "the Evil Genius of the Negro Race."[5]

"The question might naturally be asked: why should Black teachers be trained any differently from white teachers?" That was how Hollis B. Frissell, Hampton's second president, decided to open his keynote at the 43rd annual National Education Association conference in Charleston, South Carolina. It was 1900, and the audience of educators was sitting there, sweating in the sweltering ninety-degree weather, trying to keep focused as they baked like Cornish hens in the southern summer heat.

Frissell was eager to make his case. He recounted the early days of freedom when well-meaning northern educators had rushed South, bringing with them their liberal ideals. They believed that all Black Americans needed was access to the same opportunities that their white counterparts had been given. In Frissell's view, this approach had been a disaster.

Rather than blaming his northern colleagues outright, Frissell pointed to something more "scientific." He cited recent studies that claimed different races were biologically different and therefore required different treatment. "While we realize that there are certain qualities that are common to all members of the human race," he told the crowd, "it is absurd to try to make an Anglo-Saxon out of a Latin."

Frissell's ideas about Africa were equally ridiculous. According to him, the "tropical climate" of the continent had prevented its people from developing a strong work ethic over the centuries. In his mind, Black people just hadn't reached the same level of "civilization" or intelligence as white people. They weren't quite there yet—certainly not when it came to things like commerce or politics.

In his summation, educating Black children the same way white children were would only cause harm. It would fill Black people's heads with ideas about achieving the same kinds of lives as white people. To Frissell, the idea of living among a bunch of "uppity" Black folks, daring to dream of more, was downright unsettling. "Many Southern men, seeing these results, have concluded that all education of the Blacks is a failure," he said. "The mistake was not in giving them education, but in giving them the wrong *kind* of education."

Frissell wasn't just pulling these ideas out of thin air. He had been deeply influenced by a new crop of sociologists that gave legitimacy to his beliefs. And at the center of this intellectual movement was one of the leading voices in the new social science.

★ ★ ★

Franklin Giddings is considered one of the fathers of American sociology and was the head of the newly formed sociology department at Columbia University. He played a major role in shaping the way people thought about racial differences during the early 1900s, and unfortunately, a lot of his ideas stuck around for way too long.

One of Giddings's most well-known theories was something he called "consciousness of kind." Basically, he believed that people naturally feel a connection and a sense of belonging with those who are similar to them. In his words, it's "a state of consciousness in which any being, whether low or high in the scale of life, recognizes another conscious being as of like kind with itself." In simpler terms: birds of a feather flock together. He wrote several textbooks on the subject, allowing his ideas to be cemented in the minds of young college students across the country.

In his 1898 book *The Elements of Sociology: A Textbook for Colleges and Schools*, he explained that because of this "consciousness of kind," "the white man, as a general thing, is glad that the men about him also are white men; and white men often entertain feelings not altogether agreeable towards groups of black men with which they are obliged to have much contact." His thinking was heavily influenced by the English sociologist Herbert Spencer (the man who coined "survival of the fittest") and statistician Karl Pearson, who was a student of the founder of eugenics. Giddings saw racial hierarchy as a natural, biological fact.[6]

He even went as far as to justify the so-called white man's burden, claiming, "It is necessary for the higher in many ways to sustain the lower; otherwise it would be impossible for two very different races to live together." And then he twisted the knife by saying that "the same amount of educational effort does not yield equal results when applied to different stocks."

Giddings's ideas weren't just buried in textbooks—they had a real impact. His scholarship echoed in the speeches and talking points used in politics and industry. His work gave scientific credibility to the idea that Black people and other marginalized groups were inherently inferior.[7] One of Giddings's most influential moves was blending social Darwinism with statistics. He used data to try to measure the supposed evolutionary advancement—or lack thereof—of different human groups.

Giddings was a conservative man with deep family roots in Connecticut, and he made it clear that the "Anglo-Saxon" was his people. His kind. When he moved to New York City in the late 1800s, he was horrified by what he saw as an invasion of undesirable ethnic groups. To him, Italian immigrants, the Irish, Catholics, Jews—they all represented groups that hadn't yet reached the heights of the White Anglo-Saxon Protestant (WASP). His fears about his beloved America being invaded by these immigrants fueled much of his research.

But his theories also stretched far beyond New York City. He used his work to justify white colonial rule in Africa, writing in his 1906 text, *Readings in Descriptive and Historical Sociology*, that the peoples of the "heat belt"—which he used to refer to just about every place in the world except Europe, Japan, Australia, and the US—had contributed "nothing whatever to what we understand by human advancement." According to Giddings, these people hadn't produced engineers, chemists, biologists, or artists of any significance.[8]

This way of thinking became the hallmark of Columbia sociology during his time. Giddings wove together social Darwinism, racial statistics, democracy, and empire into a single social scientific theory. At its heart, his theory affirmed the supposed superiority of his version of white folks.

Giddings's theories didn't just appeal to academics—they seeped into the minds of leaders like President Frissell, shaping how they saw the world and, more dangerously, how they approached Black education. Frissell knew he couldn't get Giddings himself to come to Hampton. So he went after his star student.

★ ★ ★

Thomas Jesse Jones arrived at Hampton Institute in 1904, stepping onto a campus that had grown far beyond its humble beginnings under Mary Smith Peake's oak tree. By then, Hampton boasted sixty buildings, including dorms, a chapel, and countless training facilities for agriculture, domestic service, and other manual trades. The school's newspaper, *The Southern Workman*, proudly chronicled this growth, celebrating the expansion from its founding in 1868 to a campus that could accommodate twelve hundred students. That included a small group of Native American students, making up about 10 percent of the student body.

President Frissell personally invited Jones, a protégé of Franklin Giddings and one of the first graduates of Columbia's sociology PhD program, to join the faculty. He happily accepted, joining the all-white faculty at Hampton tasked with shaping Black minds. His own beliefs about Black education lined up perfectly with the Tuskegee Machine agenda.

Born in 1873 on the Isle of Anglesey, Wales, Jones grew up in a working-class, Cymerag-speaking family. His father was a saddler, his mother a local innkeeper. Tragedy struck when his father died unexpectedly when Jones was just eight years old, and a few years later, his family migrated to Ohio to join his mother's extended relatives.

Despite his own inconvenient origins—his Welsh accent, working-class background, and tawny complexion made it impossible for him to fully claim an Anglo-Saxon identity—Jones threw himself into American life. He earned degrees from Marietta College in Ohio and Washington and Lee University in Virginia, then went on to Union Theological Seminary for his divinity degree, and finally, Columbia for his PhD in sociology.

Jones's dissertation, *The Sociology of a New York City Block*, reflected both Giddings's teachings and Jones's internal conflict. It examined Jewish and Italian families living in tenement buildings on one Upper East Side block, assessing their "social mind and character."[9] Jones believed these immigrants desperately needed reform and assimilation, and his study reflected his unease with how much of himself he saw in them. Quietly, he recognized his own background in their lives—the outsider, the one struggling to fit into an Anglo-Saxon world. And yet, he doubled down on his belief in racial hierarchies, writing, "Every possible agency should be used to change the numerous foreign types into the Anglo-Saxon ideal."

He went on to argue that each ethnic group needed a different kind of education, shaped by their biological "limitations." He concluded that it was a mistake to teach Jewish and Italian children in the same way because of their inherent differences, believing they should be educated in separate schools with tailored curricula that fit their supposed abilities.

Jones's dissertation echoed the pseudoscientific beliefs of his time, mirroring the ideas of his mentor. Giddings, a staunch advocate of using statistics to measure human "evolution," passed down these skills to Jones, who would go on to apply them to his work with Black people in America and Africa for the next fifty years.

Jones's internalized sense of inferiority only fueled his commitment to these racist ideologies, justifying his role in shaping education for people he deemed lesser—even though he never truly saw himself as equal to the Anglo-Saxon elite he so admired.

He had been recruited to Hampton to be a change agent, and his first task was to overhaul the curriculum. "Possibly the most impressive contribution in the sociological course at Hampton," Jones proudly wrote, "is the realization of the truth that beyond differences in physique, in economic possessions, and in literacy, there are other vital differences in the dispositions, mental characteristics, and social organizations of races."

Jones wasted no time in updating the coursework with the most up-to-date "research." As part of a massive campaign to reshape Hampton's educational model, he published his teaching philosophy in a five-part essay series titled "Social Studies in the Hampton Curriculum" in the school's magazine, *The Southern Workman*. This publication served as propaganda for the Tuskegee Machine, catering to the interests of northern donors.

He assigned his Black students' readings from textbooks by Giddings and other like-minded sociologists of the time. His goal? To teach Black and Native American students their place in society. He proposed that these groups needed a slow, carefully managed dose of social reform under the guidance of white leadership.

Jones approached his classroom like a social experiment, treating his students as lab rats to be studied and categorized. He adorned his lessons with charts, graphs, quotes from academic authorities, and statistics, applying quantitative methods to his study of what he saw as "infantile races."

It wasn't long before Jones established himself as an expert on the American Negro. He lived among Black students at Hampton, observed their ways, and used these experiences to reinforce his belief that it was his divine duty to chart the course for Black futures.

For Jones, the harsh reality he imposed on his Black students was simple: their struggles weren't the fault of white supremacy but the result of their own nature. His goal was to convince his students that their status as second-class citizens wasn't something they could—or should—fight. Instead, they were to accept it as the natural order of things.

I am sad to say that this kind of low-key racism is still taught in many classrooms to our kids today. Black students are disproportionately disciplined, being four times more likely to be suspended than their white peers. Behaviors such as asking a lot of questions or exhibiting high energy—often seen as curiosity or perhaps attention deficit hyperactivity disorder in white students—are frequently misinterpreted as defiance in Black students, leading to harsher punishments. Further, harmful narratives that academically successful Black kids are simply "acting white" has perpetuated damaging stereotypes, discouraging them from excelling due to fear of social isolation or bullying. Moreover, pseudoscientific theories still prevail. The discredited "bell-curve" hypothesis proposes that Black kids are biologically just not as intelligent as their white counterparts. Although debunked, such ideas have left a lingering impact, influencing perceptions and expectations of Black youth at their own schools.[10]

Not long into his Hampton appointment, the US Census Bureau invited Thomas Jesse Jones to serve as the lead statistician for a special project in the upcoming 1910 Census. His job was to gather facts on the state of Black Americans for the official government report.

The federal government, along with many white Americans, was becoming increasingly anxious about what seemed to be the early stages of a mass migration of Black people from the South to cities in the North and Midwest.

They didn't yet have the language we use today. "Urban" wasn't synonymous with "Black," and cities like Detroit and Chicago hadn't yet become iconic "chocolate cities." But something was brewing, and white southerners were alarmed by how many Black folks were leaving town. Meanwhile, white northerners were noticing more Black faces on their city streets every day.

The bureau saw the 1910 Census as a way to make sense of what was happening. Jones's findings would influence how the government viewed Black people's lives and needs. The census is a tool the government uses to make critical decisions about resource allocation, policymaking, and the overall welfare of its citizens. And it's not just the government that uses census data. Academics, activists, advocates, philanthropies, and policymakers rely on it too. So having someone like Jones at the helm, a man whose views were shaped by his belief in racial hierarchies and scientific racism, was ominous, to say the least. The government might have abandoned its responsibility to its Black citizens in most ways, but here they were letting Jones define their reality in cold, hard numbers.

Within a year, Jones's responsibilities expanded yet again, and he was promoted to director of the Division of Racial Groups. Like a modern-day overseer, his new role not only kept African Americans under his watch but also placed the lives of American Indians and Mexican Americans under his purview.

Jones had always dreamed bigger than being just a faculty member at Hampton. His ambitions stretched far beyond scraping his way up the educational ladder for the next twenty years.

To fit into the high-class society he so admired, Jones worked on scrubbing away the traces of his humble roots. He clipped the elongated, singsong vowels of his southern Welsh accent and would often make self-deprecating jokes about his "swarthy" skin at dinner parties to ease the discomfort of the elite company he kept. No number of degrees or amount of performative whiteness could fully erase the inconvenient stain of his ethnicity. But with shrewd determination and some luck, Jones managed to align himself with men of power and prestige. All he needed was a little bit of stardust to take him the rest of the way.

Around the time Jones was building his reputation as an expert on Black education, Booker T. Washington hired Robert Ezra Park to be his right-hand man. Park, a white Jewish man who had bounced from career to career—from journalism to philosophy—became Washington's special assistant and publicist. Essentially, his job was to know Washington better than Washington knew himself.

He had to anticipate Washington's desires, frustrations, fears, and ambitions, and make sure everything that went public kept Washington in the best light. Park even ghostwrote three of Washington's books and was the pen behind many of Washington's speeches and op-eds.

But Park wasn't content to stay in the shadows forever. Like Jones, he had bigger plans.

In 1912, Park's and Jones's time at Tuskegee and Hampton, respectively, ended. They both applied for the same job at the newly created Phelps-Stokes Fund in New York City. Caroline Stokes, a wealthy New York heiress, had founded the philanthropy as part of her will before she died. The foundation's mission was to promote "the education of negroes, both in Africa and the United States, North American Indians, and needy and deserving white students." What made the Phelps-Stokes Fund stand out was its international scope—it wasn't just focused on the US; it also wanted to meddle in African affairs.

The foundation's board members made it clear: they wanted a social scientist for the job. Frissell, of course, threw his full support behind Jones. In a letter to the trustees, he highlighted Jones's government connections, arguing that his ties to the Census Bureau would be a huge asset to the foundation. Frissell even took a subtle jab at Park, saying that Jones was a better fit than "someone connected with a Church board, or closely tied to a particular school." The trustees agreed, and Jones landed the job. For Jones, it was a major win—beating out Park felt like hitting a game-winning shot in the clutch.

Meanwhile, Park didn't waste time feeling sorry for himself. He resigned from Tuskegee and set off for Chicago, where he joined a group of scholars who were studying the city's social problems in Black and immigrant communities. It wasn't long before Park became a key figure in what would later be known as the "Chicago School of Sociology," transforming the city into a hub for sociological research.

Back in New York, Jones was settling into his new role. His combination of academic training, government connections, and passion for social reform made him a powerful weapon for the Tuskegee Machine. He quickly became a major force in shaping the direction for the future of Black education, not just in the US but globally.

Unlike Booker T. Washington, who built his power through charm and political savvy, Jones used his academic credentials and feigned scientific objectivity to climb to the top. Through their roles at Tuskegee and Hampton, and later at places like Chicago and the Phelps-Stokes Fund, men like Robert Ezra Park and Thomas Jesse Jones became the ones who defined Black life—at least in the eyes of white institutions. Their time at Hampton and Tuskegee wasn't just work. It was bootcamp. They were sharpening their sociological tools for the next phase of this battle over the Black mind.

CHAPTER 9

Changing of the Guard

Margaret Murray Washington breathed slow and shallow. If she remained still, she would wake up from this dizzying nightmare, but in the near thirty-hour train ride to New York numbness soaked into the marrow of her bones, and she began to accept that Booker T. Washington was at death's door. Twice the widower himself, it was now his turn to leave her behind. Her only resolve was to bring her husband back home to the red clay dirt of the South while the breath remained in his body.

He visited New York regularly to call on business of various sorts—donor meetings, press interviews, and his fervent lectures proselytizing the promise of industrial education. On a particularly cool day, November 5, 1915, Washington decided to play hooky to visit his friends, William G. Wilcox and Seth Low. The men swaggered throughout the streets of Manhattan as if they had keys to the city in their back pockets. In many ways, they did.

Seth Low was a distinguished man of family wealth and accomplishment who earned his high social standing many times over on the New York scene. He was a former diplomat who had served three terms as mayor of Brooklyn and New York City, and a short stint as Columbia University's eleventh president. Like Wilcox, Seth Low also served on the Tuskegee board of trustees. While Tuskegee had brought the three men into one another's orbit, they were visionaries who shared sensibilities and interests about future-proofing the American economy through education.

What should have been a leisurely afternoon walk felt like the toll of a year's worth of hard labor on Washington's body. His friends noticed the effusive bursts of sweat streaming from his clammy, sallow skin. Surmising that he was dehydrated or had a bout of food poisoning, they ushered their weary mate to a private doctor's office close by in Midtown Manhattan. The room shrank when Dr. Bastedo shared the devastating prognosis that Washington's kidneys were failing. He had but days to live.

Low's shock turned to anger. With a tightened jaw and narrowed eyes, he scoffed at the news and sent it back, as though he were at a restaurant. With his bourgeoise upbringing, he wasn't accustomed to openly showing his distress, and only did so by exerting his wealth. Low and Wilcox arranged a private suite for Washington uptown at St. Luke's Hospital, where he could be seen by the best surgeons the city had to offer. Yet, nothing could stop it; Washington was actively dying.[1]

Margaret breathed a sigh of relief when she arrived at the hospital to find her husband still conscious. Accompanied by their Black family doctor, Dr. John Kenney, they boarded a private railroad car on the back of the segregated train to make their way home to Alabama. From slavery to freedom to his meteoric rise to fame, Washington had remained loyal to the Southern soil. "I was born in the

South, have lived all my life in the South, and expect to die and be buried in the South," he'd declared.

The Washingtons arrived at the Tuskegee train station on November 13. Twelve hours later, at 4:40 a.m., he was gone.

As the sun set over the imposing rock that marked his grave at his beloved Tuskegee Institute, Booker T. Washington's legacy became etched into the annals of American history. Founded in 1881 with Washington at its helm, the Tuskegee Institute stood as a sibling institution to an ideology, the "Hampton-Tuskegee model of industrial education," a doctrine to which he lent not just his support but his very image and essence as its representative. His 1895 Atlanta Compromise speech catapulted him onto the national stage, and from then on, he was knighted by white America as the undisputed leader of the Negro race. The power and sway he held penetrated Black institutions, programs, lives, and careers in overt and indetectable ways. He had, for the past twenty years, been the central processing unit of the Tuskegee Machine.

Schools and monuments bearing his name are peppered across the country. A library of biographies—sixteen in total—chronicle his life and work, one of which earned the illustrious Pulitzer Prize. Born enslaved in Virginia, Washington lived through the triumph of Civil War, the devastating failure of Reconstruction, and the unjust system of Jim Crow. Doors to white institutions, otherwise bolt locked to African Americans, flew open for him. In 1896, for instance, President Theodore Roosevelt invited Washington to dine with his family, making him the first African American dinner guest at the White House—an event that sparked ire and vitriol in the white press.

Decades later, however, Washington's death sent a wave of shock and reverence throughout the nation.

"The death of Mr. Washington marks an epoch in the history of America. He was the greatest Negro leader since Frederick Douglass, and the most distinguished man, white or black, who has come out of the South since the Civil War," wrote W. E. B. Du Bois in *The Crisis*. Irrespective of their deep-seated differences, the good doctor had to give Washington his props. Similarly, President Roosevelt said, "He was one of the distinguished citizens of the United States. . . . I mourn his loss, and feel that one of the most useful citizens of our land has gone."

Washington's praise, however, was clouded by criticism of his educational agenda. The socialist newspaper *New York Call* openly expressed disappointment that Washington never truly fought for fundamental rights like citizenship, education, or self-determination for Black people. Washington's role in the disenfranchisement of Black Americans led to the decline of Black colleges and the strengthening of a racial caste system.

Washington's life continues to perplex biographers and the public.[2] It was filled with awe-inspiring achievements and underscored by deleterious compromise and power mongering. Washington moved across the barriers of the color line like a man with a magic key to the world's most impenetrable lock. Sadly, he often used that key to lock the doors of liberation behind him, shutting out his own people.

When Washington passed away, an era in Black education came to an end. He was the spokesperson for the notion that Black people should pull themselves up by the bootstraps and strive for economic prosperity, while eschewing civil rights and equal citizenship. His sudden death caused a shift within the Tuskegee Machine, as its influence would no longer be tied to one powerful man. Like a caterpillar transforming into a butterfly, the machine took on a new form and greater abilities.

★ ★ ★

In a well-appointed alcove in 1 Rockefeller Plaza, a specter of power and wealth lingered in the air of a boardroom two weeks after Washington's death. A clandestine group of men, both white and Black, sat in a room shrouded in conspiracy. The time to mourn was over. They were convened to strategize the future of Black education after Washington. Among them were the powerful, the affluent, and the opportunists—those who saw the Tuskegee Machine as a vehicle for social climbing and cozying up one's proximity to power. They were all men, save for one stenographer pressed against the walls alongside the carefully curated pieces of rare Asian art from the Rockefeller's vast collection. It is because of her that a transcript exists today of this most surreptitious meeting.[3]

Thomas Jesse Jones, a key player in the group and now a representative of the Phelps-Stokes Fund, took the lead. He urged the group to create a public relations strategy to ease Black peoples' concerns about a caste system. He proposed to rebrand the Southern education movement with Black leaders at the forefront or to add a bit of science to the curriculum to placate the concerns of Black communities.

Jones had spent the last two years exploring the hills and hollers of the South, observing every Black school and Black teacher for his forthcoming work of pseudoscience on behalf of his employer, the Phelps-Stokes Fund.

Abraham Flexner, Carnegie Corporation and the Rockefeller Foundation trustee, argued that the idea of racial equality was "the worst reason in the world" to "force" Black children to meet the educational standards of white children. It was a paternalistic narrative, one that justified the segregation and control of Black education under the guise of helping.

At the time, there were only sixty-four public high schools for Black students in the entire South, and some states, like Georgia, had just one. To make matters worse, public expenditures for Black segregated schools were one-tenth that of white schools in some states, even though Black workers paid local taxes to support the school systems in their communities.[4] As a result of the South's decision to abdicate its responsibility to educate *all* children within state borders, most Black schools chose to remain private and independent like Lucy Craft Laney's school in Augusta.

The consensus among the group was that these schools should be left to fail, starved of the financial support necessary to survive.

However, they faced a significant challenge. Hampton and Tuskegee were only equipped to train elementary school teachers. This left these school's graduates unprepared to take on high school teaching or leadership roles, a gap that could weaken their control. Even Dr. B. T. Williams, an African American professor at Hampton, acknowledged that "skill with their hands" alone would not allow Black teachers to lead.

Jones insisted that Black educators were not always "sympathetic" to the Hampton model and that Black people had a deep distrust of the Tuskegee Machine.

Dr. John Hope, president of Morehouse College and an advocate for liberal education, argued that Black people wanted an education that allowed them to fully compete in American society, not one that relegated them to second-class status. But Hope's words fell on deaf ears. The chair, Dr. Hollis B. Frissell, looked past Hope to

Jones, asking if there was any truth to what had just been said. Jones and the others doubled down on their assertion. Frissell reaffirmed Hampton's commitment to manual skills over academic pursuits, signaling that their focus would remain unchanged.

Washington's death set off a race to answer the big questions of the day: Would Black people become full citizens or remain second-class subjects? What was the plan, and who would lead it? The powerful figures behind the Tuskegee Machine understood this moment perfectly. Jones knew that controlling Black minds was the key to controlling Black bodies. What could no longer be done with whips and chains would now have to be done through education. But they weren't the only ones who realized this. There was another meeting happening uptown.

In a lavish Upper East Side apartment, the NAACP chair Du Bois and his most trusted confidant, Joel Spingarn, devised a plan for a political reset. Spingarn could be bold and unhinged at times, yet he was conscious of his positionality as a white and Jewish man in this debate. Like siblings conspiring to bring their squabbling parents back together, the two men devised a plan to get Black leaders to come together now that Washington's dominance had ended; dukes down and armor off.

They decided a new retreat might be helpful, leading to what would become known as the Amenia Conference.[5] Black leaders convened at Spingarn's 250-acre country estate at Troutbeck, nestled in the rolling hills of Amenia, New York. Spingarn was clear that it needed to be an independent gathering with the goal of providing a safe and luxurious space to find common ground and make peace.

The male guests arrived in three or four groups. However, unlike the Tuskegee Machine meeting at Rockefeller Plaza, there'd be women present—and not just as notetakers either.

Now in her sixties, Lucy Craft Laney approached the green pastures at Troutbeck with measured steps. Her gait slightly uneven from the wear and tear put on her knees and hips from years of traveling like a door-to-door salesperson raising money for her school. Her coffee-brown face still round and jovial but bearing the lines of a woman who had seen some things. She took a deep breath, full of hope, as she entered.

She had been assigned to room with an old friend and fellow educator, Mary Church Terrell. The ladies were thrilled to see each other. Thankful not to be alone with all the male ego that was destined to suffocate the room.

However, not all were thrilled to see one another. Years of political contention had left many relationships strained. But over shared meals and walks in nature's beauty, the coldness between attendees began to thaw.

The split between Washington and Du Bois had made it tough for Black leaders to navigate the contentious landscape of Black education. Each had to pick a side, and the path forward for Black progress spiraled. Efforts to advance the race were sabotaged through letters and whispers and private discussions scurrilously leaked to the press. Black leaders suffered a long-standing battle that had taken root in Black political circles and was now affecting the lives of their children's education.

Over time, their arguments and positions became so rigid that no one would give in. The pursuit of being right and winning had blinded them from the original goal of freedom, equality, and full citizenship in a country built on their ancestors' blood. Beneath the political battles lay hurt feelings and deep distrust traced back to the Tuskegee Machine's divide-and-conquer tactics that helped fuel the Du Bois–Washington divide.

Du Bois later reflected on how challenging it was to arrange such a meeting, with delicate decisions about who should be invited and how to navigate lingering "hurts and enmities."

Now, in 1916, after decades in the trenches, these veteran warriors gathered. If not full unity, at least a truce was needed.

The assembly's guests reflected the diversity of Black thought. Attendees included HBCU presidents like John Hope and Robert Russa Moton. The best of Black America's writers and religious leaders, including Charles Chesnutt and Bishop John Hurst, made up the gathering's distinguished roster of fifty African American leaders.

The sense of common ground was facilitated by the careful program crafted by Spingarn and Du Bois. Aiming to foster unity rather than division, the coconspirators curated an agenda that allowed all voices to be heard and, perhaps for the first time in a long time, understood—no matter what "side" they had previously been on. Topics in the conference consisted of "Colored Youth in the Leading Universities" on day one, "Practical Separation" on the next, and "The Practical Paths" on the third and final day. Each day was structured by a morning roundtable, a formal midday session, and a night roundtable. Du Bois and Spingarn selected people whose politics lay on both sides of the shrinking divide to mediate. As they navigated weighted discussions, their senses were titillated by an orchestra of pastel blooms in manicured cottage gardens, the earthy scent of pine along quiet hiking trails, the cool lake water, and a smorgasbord of chef-prepared delicacies to delight the palate.

When the discussions became intense, they took breaks for outdoor games, swimming, and hikes through the enchanted forests aligning the Hudson River valley. They all wanted the same basic things—economic opportunity, voting rights, law enforcement, and the right to fulsome Black life—though the paths to achieving them diverged widely.

The conference attendees pledged to keep the intimate details of their discussions private. Presidents Hope and Moton, men who held opposing views, conducted sessions. But this time, both sides had the opportunity to be heard and understood before they went back out into the white world.

The Amenia Conference marked a turning point, where the possibility of moving beyond old divisions was palpable, offering a path forward for the pursuit of Black freedom dreams with a newfound solidarity. It was a rare event of clarity and mutual understanding that, as Du Bois would later reflect, prepared the race for the challenges ahead.

The Black united front developed at the Amenia Conference did not last long. Months after the conference, the United States entered World War I, and all hell broke loose.

CHAPTER 10

All Hell

Philanthropy-funded studies have historically influenced policies that deeply impact Black lives. World War I launched a slew of studies in the early twentieth century, like *Negro Education*, *The American Dilemma*, and the Moynihan Report, that were funded by either the government or private philanthropies, and had lasting effects.

The Moynihan Report, published by the US Department of Labor, concluded that Black families were struggling because Black women were "emasculating" Black men, driving Black fathers from the home. This study had a major influence on policies related to welfare and housing, creating decades of damaging narratives and policies affecting Black families. In addition to shaping public opinion, government and philanthropic studies like these acted as a directory for funding decisions—who gets what, and why. Therefore, it is important for Black people to know the role that studies like these continue to play.

Negro Education marked the beginning of a long history of such studies, and it had a major effect on Black schools in the South.

★ ★ ★

At the pinnacle of his career as philanthropic agent for the Phelps-Stokes Fund, with Booker T. Washington out of the way, Thomas Jesse Jones seized the mantle. His *Negro Education* study unleashed a disinformation campaign on Black schools—first here in the US and later in South Africa.

Negro Education: A Study of Private and Higher Schools for Colored People in the United States debuted as the most comprehensive study of Black education in the nation.[1] After five years of scouring every Black community in the South, the Phelps-Stokes Fund study was finally published. Thomas Jesse Jones and his team of researchers—Tipton Ray Snavely, Thomas Jack Woofter, and Ocea Taylor—had personally visited 790 Black private schools. They collected thousands of pages of survey data accounting for every building and bolt on each campus. Line by line, they reviewed each page of each school's curriculum, interviewed most teachers and every principal, and observed classes. The team held court with local whites in every southern community to take their temperature on the idea of "colored schools." Jones employed every statistical method in his toolbelt to present his feelings as facts.

During his time at the census, Jones had curried favor with the sitting commissioner of education for the US Board of Education, P. P. Claxton—a white southern man of Tennessee roots and predilections. In his capacity as a federal official, he felt it his duty to support the study as a matter of national economic interest. Jones argued that "the importance of the investigation is indicated by the number of agencies expressing a strong desire that a 'Who's Who' in Negro education be ascertained."

Northern foundations, industrialists, and wealthy donors—all the king's horses and all the king's men—had been beating down Jones's door to do something to help them sift the wheat from the tears of Black institutions. In addition, Commissioner Claxton admitted that he was beginning to receive demands from "Northern friends of the Negro" who were becoming increasingly suspicious of numerous schools seeking aid. The information provided by Jones's study would solve his problem.

This study, carried out by a team of social scientists, would serve as a directory to identify which Black schools were worthy of white dollars.

A good ole government study is supposed to start out objective. However, Jones and his team set foot in the South to begin research for which they'd predetermined the findings. Outlined in the confidential "lines of investigation" of the memorandum of understanding was a charge to support the "adaptation of the school to the needs of the community from which pupils are received." In a time when Black southerners were living under a regime of terror and exclusion, it would be to no one's surprise what those needs of the community would be. The study was to emphasize on the "moral, mental, and manual" elements of education and a focus on teacher training in that mode.

On November 14, 1912, the Phelps-Stokes Fund entered a secret agreement with the US Bureau of Education to publish the study as though it were its own. To paper the deal, Jones and his team were to receive a nominal salary of one dollar from the agency, technically making them official government employees. On the back end, the Phelps-Stokes Fund would pay all the real salaries and travel expenses associated with the study. Furthermore, the Phelps-Stokes Fund would be acknowledged on the front page of the study as a collaborator. In the end, both parties would get what they wanted—an iron-clad strategy to checkmate the battle for the Black mind once and for all.

A study published as an official document of the federal Bureau of Education gave *Negro Education* a gravitas and air of impartiality.

And having that research carried out by the nation's leading white social scientist lent it the legitimacy as an authoritative work of scientific inquiry, not ideology.

Prior to its publication, Jones consulted privately with the US Bureau of Labor, the presidents of Hampton and Tuskegee, as well as the trustees of Rockefeller Foundation and Carnegie Corporation and other big philanthropies. Through these behind-the-scenes moves, Jones and the Tuskegee Machine had stacked the deck in their favor. Black educators who dared to defy the study's recommendations found themselves cast as unarmed Davids squaring up against an army of Goliaths.

Knowing they needed to keep the conspiracy under the radar, the Tuskegee Machine's network of power brokers agreed publicly to play nice in the sand. Jones prepared talking points for those involved. Philanthropic trustees agreed to sing the bureau's praises for embarking on such a monumental endeavor, signaling their approval of a neutral federal entity taking charge of such an important national issue. This signaled their consensus and helped mask the orchestrated collaboration behind the scenes.

The fall Augusta air offered just the right balance in the crosswinds of the cool river breeze and sticky heat. As Jones and his team approached the campus at Haines Normal and Industrial Institute, a wave of students bustled across grounds like a decadent sprinkle of chocolate drops. Their brown faces were bright and ready for school, exuding a curiosity and joy that stood out to the distant observers.

By October 1913, the educational seeds that Miss Lucy had planted at her school had grown into a forest of knowledge and culture. Haines now boasted a student population of 860 pupils. Students flocked to its campus from near and far, with some boarding students hailing from out of state to access a quality education. The school delivered a curriculum that even rivaled some New England boarding schools.

With only twenty-two faculty members, the Haines Normal and Industrial Institute offered a full-suite education, from kindergarten all the way through high school. Jones, however, found the school's name quite duplicitous. Although Miss Lucy's school included the word *industrial* in its title, intention of that term appeared to lie at the periphery of what was happening on the ground. "The secondary course requires English, 4 years; mathematics, 4; and history, 3," Jones reported in the insidious *Negro Education* study. What really irritated Jones' sensibilities was as follows: "Elective subjects included: Latin taken by 91 pupils; French, taken by 31; German, 26; Greek, 17; psychology, 21; physics, 16; physiology, 14; chemistry, 9; history and civics, 19; sociology, 6." To his disappointment, only two teachers offered courses in manual training or gardening. He noted that the industrial courses at the school were inadequate.

Jones and his team found themselves in a loop of cognitive dissonance.

Nearly thirty years in the game, Haines had a proven track record of student success. Alumni attended colleges nationwide, including historically Black *and* white institutions. They had become Black entrepreneurs, teachers, hairdressers, nurses, doctors, musicians, chefs—you name it. Haines alumni pride was strong and enduring in cities across the country. "Laney Clubs" were organized as fundraising engines to support the continued work of their precious alma mater.

In *Negro Education*, Jones had no choice but to give Haines her props, citing the school's effective management and acknowledging that "the wise administration of the principal has won for the school the confidence of both white and colored people."

However, Jones's final recommendations in *Negro Education* suggested reducing the school's emphasis on foreign languages. He advised that Haines focus on teacher training and "elementary" science—code for domestic work—and recommended that "the courses in theory and practice of gardening and simple manual training be strengthened."

As a backhanded compliment, Jones wrote to his boss advocating that the Phelps-Stokes Fund grant Haines Institute funds "for the encouragement of gardening."

Over the next three years, they visited every Black private school in the South. Like bumblebees buzzing from flower to flower, they went back to these institutions again and again. An education conference in New York, school visits in Florida, team huddles at the home office in Washington, DC, then quiet meetings with trustees—this was a normal month's travel for the research team about to better implement the plan to return Black students to field work.

Jones made sure to keep his boss and financier Anson Phelps Stokes updated on every detail. They exchanged letters incessantly, with Jones issuing commands and authorizing or redirecting efforts. Jones understood that his power was merely a reflection of men who actually possessed it, and he showed great reverence to men like Stokes who kept him as a permanent wingman.

However, Jones had an agenda of his own. If his birthright relegated him to the status of "off-white," he intended to navigate the high seas of power on someone else's boat in a last-ditch effort to elevate his status. Even in the months leading up to Washington's death, Jones played behind-the-scenes games through strategic alliances, quiet manipulation, and ruthless gatekeeping.

May 26th, 1914

Dear Dr. Stokes,

    While at Tuskegee recently I was informed by Dr. Washington that he is very eager to have you become one of the trustees of the Tuskegee Institute. At the time of the conversation, it seemed to me desirable that you accept the responsibility. On second thought I am wondering what the effect of your acceptance would have on the recommendation of our study.

    Already I am compelled to guard against the impression that I am carrying out a propaganda for Tuskegee and Hampton. It occurs to me that your acceptance of this intimate relationship to Tuskegee may be interpreted as evidence that we are unduly favorable to industrial education.

Sincerely,

Thomas Jesse Jones

No matter how much he tried to distance himself from it, the stench of bad science trailed the study at every turn. This he could not bear. Jones's value came from his singular status as an expert social scientist, an objective researcher who sought truth only through verified facts and rational analysis. To be viewed as a pay-for-play academic would derail his ascent to power and prestige.

Like an agent managing his talent, Thomas Jesse Jones kept close tabs on Anson Phelps Stokes. He learned his quirks and preferences, flooding him with letters filled with the smallest details of his interactions in the field. But these letters often contained subtle manipulations, designed to strengthen his employer's dependency on him. Through this constant communication, he elevated himself to the role of a special adviser to Stokes, uninvitedly vetting opportunities and guarding his reputation on his boss's behalf.

Jones sowed seeds of suspicion and Black-led schools as "up to something." After his trip to South Carolina, he reported: "The dominant impression of the October trip was that made by a number of frauds which I observed during that month."

Jones was horrified to report on how widespread liberal education had become and suggested the schools needed better accounting systems. By framing Black schools as financially mismanaged and overly ambitious, Jones reinforced the narrative that white oversight was essential. His reports of chaos fueled the Tuskegee Machine's drive for complete control over Black education.

In 1913, Jones floated the idea of capturing control of the Black education system through bureaucratic tactics to Commissioner Claxton. He suggested that the Phelps-Stokes Fund, under the Bureau of Education's authority, become the mandated financial auditor for every Black school in the South.

He proudly suggested "entering wedges" to disrupt the organization and cooperation between Black schools.

Most of all, this allowed Jones to control the narrative.

Julius Rosenwald was the co-owner of the clothing manufacturing giant Sears, Roebuck, and Company, and a Jewish American businessman turned philanthropist who expressed a deep commitment to the advancement of African American education. Persuaded by William H. Baldwin and Booker T. Washington, Rosenwald was sold on the premise of an industrial education model adapted specifically for Black Americans. Inviting him into the Machine's inner circle, Washington extended to Rosenwald a seat on Tuskegee's board of trustees, a position he held from 1912 until his death.

The mega-millionaire began to consult with Black communities to discuss their needs and to support building new schoolhouses throughout the South through matching grants, pledging to match any amount raised by the community. This sent Jones into a frenzy.

Jones always walked the line between flattery and manipulation. He would suggest without commanding, inform without fully revealing. Like a skilled puppet master, he played both sycophant and manipulator, depending on the moment. His tactics were subtle—opening his reports with praise and enthusiasm before slyly introducing seeds of doubt, much like how he intercepted Anson Phelps Stokes from accepting a position on the Tuskegee board.

The study, published in 1917 by the US Bureau of Education, spanned a two-volume tome including charts, graphs, analyses, and recommendations. It also included a full directory of each of the 790 schools, with a brief assessment and set of recommendations for each institution. Except for a set of brief opening remarks, the remaining eleven hundred pages were penned by Thomas Jesse Jones.

In his preamble to *Negro Education*, Commissioner Claxton framed the educational issue as not only detrimental to Black people but as harmful to the South as a whole, arguing that an underdeveloped Black population hindered white progress.

Jones saw the problem of Black education as a matter to be resolved by white America, where white management and guidance were essential for Black progress.

Throughout the report, Jones portrayed Black Americans as a people in need of rescue, seduced by ideals of racial equality and distracted by "book-learning" that centered foreign languages and highbrow intellectual pursuits that were irrelevant to their societal roles. He expressed disdain for Black aspirations and criticized the desire among Black leaders for higher education.

This was brought on by noble yet naive ideals of racial equality carried south by northern whites and the white South's refusal to expend tax dollars on schools for freed people of any kind. This was bad for America, Black and white.

Nearly 90 percent of Black Americans were living under the terror of Jim Crow. They were citizens but could neither vote nor serve on a jury of their peers. They were being deployed in Europe to deliver military service during World War I in defense of freedom and democracy, while lynching abounded with impunity at home in their southern towns. Out of 961,887 Black kids aged fifteen to nineteen in the South, there were only sixty-four public high schools to serve them. In Black belt cities in Georgia, such as Atlanta, Augusta, Columbus, and Macon, there were none.

The absence of public schools for Black children made the work of Black private schools founded by Black educators, such as Lucy Craft Laney, Mary McLeod Bethune, and Charlotte Hawkins Brown, all the more urgent. They had no choice but to fight for Black kids to have access to education, and to travel from coast to coast, begging and borrowing in a never-ending fight to keep their schools open. The *Negro Education* study made the uphill battle so much steeper.

Jones's recommendations for K–12 schools included manual training for elementary students, mechanical practice and household arts in secondary schools, rural trades for small industrial schools, and specialized trade schools for preparing industrial teachers and tradesmen, with household arts training for women. His aim was to steer Black students away from intellectual pursuits and instead funnel them into vocational roles.

His assessment of HBCUs was damning, asserting that out of the near one hundred schools, only three were deemed worthy of being referred to as a college.

The NAACP offices bustled with activity day and night. In and out of its Fifth Avenue Greenwich Village building were activists and organizers, field agents and local chapter heads, and the executive leadership who drove the mission of one of the country's most powerful civil rights organizations for Black Americans. W. E. B. Du Bois's office was lined with thousands of books and journal articles, like bricks upholding a culture. Now, at almost fifty years old, Du Bois had taken a position as editor in chief of *The Crisis* magazine, the official news outlet of the NAACP. During his time in the position, the magazine was like an umbilical cord feeding vital information and educational content to the masses.

The Black press was the political unifying agent for African Americans in the early twentieth century. Not only did these periodicals, such as *The Chicago Defender*, *The Amsterdam News*, and *The Crisis*, enjoy broad subscribership; they also traveled on the storied trains and buses facilitating the African American Great Migration. Herein, Black people shared information about the dangers and opportunities that lie in different cities across the country and about jobs, injustices, dreams, and everything in between—the Black press covered the fullness of Black life in America.

Du Bois recognized that *Negro Education* could perpetuate harmful policies that would affect Black schools. In his review of the study, Du Bois concluded that it was "pitifully wrong," stating that "the balance between ancient thought and modern industry was crucial, and any suggestion otherwise did a grave disservice to the future of Black education."

However, the study did not catch the ire of all Black leaders. Robert Russa Moton, among those at the secret 1915 Rockefeller meeting and the Amenia Conference, supported Jones's study. Other conservative Black leaders from the Hampton-Tuskegee school, such as J. E. K. Aggrey, the West African–born professor and educationist, followed suit. Both Moton and Aggrey enjoyed various appointments on Carnegie and Rockefeller boards. In fact, many Black folks championed the Hampton Idea to their students and communities. And as we know, the study was a huge success with white educators and donors.

Things only worsened from here. Jones's study spread across Europe, landing on the desks of European colonial officials. They were impressed by what Jones was able to accomplish with *Negro Education* and his credibility as a US social scientist. His research was seen as objective, making it easier for white administrators abroad to justify underfunding and undermining Black schools abroad.

A few years after *Negro Education* was published, Jones was invited by a coalition of officials from European nations, including England and Belgium, to assess the educational needs of Black people in colonial Africa. Throughout the 1920s, Jones took his methods to South Africa, Kenya, and Rhodesia. He built relationships with white educationists in South Africa and negotiated board positions for them with the Carnegie Corporation and Rockefeller Foundation.

By the end of the decade, many of the same philanthropies that had stirred chaos across the Black educational landscape in the United States had extended their operations to the African continent. Before these countries even had the chance to develop real school systems, Jones and the Phelps-Stokes Fund got involved, pushing their will on Black minds in harmful ways.

In my research, it is heartbreaking to see the letters written by Black educators literally begging for support from philanthropists like the Carnegie Corporation, the General Education Board, and the Phelps-Stokes Fund.

The Harvard-educated historian Carter G. Woodson, in one of his last publications before his death, reflected on the devastating impact that the Phelps-Stokes Fund had on Black schools and educators. He said that by the time Black educators realized what was happening, they had been shut out without even knowing it.[2] Black educators were aware of the challenges they faced, but they had no idea just how deep the manipulation and sabotage went, led by people like "the Evil Genius of the Negro Race," Thomas Jesse Jones.

CHAPTER 11

The Eve of an Era

Despite the confines of Jim Crow, the influence of Black brilliance and creativity had become woven into the very fabric of American life. Education was at the core of this transformation. But it wasn't just about academics. Black schools were sacred spaces during this era of racial segregation. They were sanctuaries for us—places where Black culture was affirmed, celebrated, and nurtured. Segregated Black schools were centers of faith, community organizing, and self-determination. Within these walls, Black teachers crafted a unique pedagogy that spoke directly to the needs of their students. They were the first branches to sprout from the tree of knowledge that had once been forbidden to their ancestors, and they made it their mission to ensure the next generation would eat freely.

This legacy of Black pedagogy was deeply intertwined with the idea of racial uplift. Black educators—many just one generation removed from slavery—dedicated their lives to nourishing Black minds with knowledge, confidence, and self-love. They understood that education was more than a pathway to a better life; it was an act of defiance, a declaration of independence, and a tool for liberation.

And they didn't do it alone. As we learned earlier, Black educators had begun to organize, forming teachers' associations as early as 1903. Over time, these organizations grew in power and influence, and by 1923, Mary McLeod Bethune had become president of the National Association of Teachers in Colored Schools.

Under her leadership, the organization flourished. Bethune understood the power of community outreach. She launched *The Bulletin*, a public-facing news outlet that kept everyday Black communities engaged with the happenings of their schools. *The Bulletin* was a lifeline, sharing news about the needs of Black children, the struggles of Black teachers, and the achievements of Black students. It shone a light on the importance of creating affirming school environments where Black students could see themselves in the curriculum.

That same year, in 1923, Mary McLeod Bethune had also made the strategic decision to merge her school with the nearby Cookman College, in an effort to stave off financial peril. She became the first president of the newly formed Bethune-Cookman College, making history as the first Black woman to lead a historically Black college or university (HBCU)—especially significant given that she had founded the school herself. Even after stepping down as president, Bethune continued to wield significant political influence behind the scenes. She led the "Black Cabinet" during Franklin D. Roosevelt's administration, using her platform to push for policies that ensured equal access and opportunity for Black Americans in education and business. Bethune-Cookman College stands today as a testament to her legacy.[1]

People like Carter G. Woodson worked closely with these associations, and in 1915, he cofounded a new organization to support Black educators and researchers—the Association for the Study of African American Life and History. In 1926, he founded Black

History Week—now Black History Month—to ensure that Black students learned about their own history, even if it wasn't officially part of the curriculum. Through what Harvard professor Jarvis Givens called "fugitive pedagogy," Woodson and other educators smuggled books and materials about Black history into classrooms, ensuring that young Black minds were exposed to a broader, more inclusive view of American history—one that recognized their contributions and affirmed their humanity.

Once again, the tides of change had come to shore. The 1930s marked a new chapter in the battle for the Black mind. Yet again, Black education was at the cusp of a transformation. The world itself was undergoing a shift as America moved into a new era of technological advancement that would redefine the fabric of everyday life. And the landscape of work and society shifted with the widespread availability of cars, modern appliances, and new forms of housing. Electricity and the assembly line redefined productivity, and with these advances, a range of new markets emerged. Radios, refrigerators, vacuum cleaners, and a host of other household items now found their way into American homes.

As the country modernized, so did its labor force. With mechanization replacing the old ways of farming and manual labor, the demand for workers skilled in those areas plummeted. This shift had a ripple effect on Black schools in the South. The well of white dollars donated to prop up industrial education began to run dry, as the value of training a Black labor force in manual work was no longer a pressing priority for those benefactors. But as one door closed, another opened. State-funded public school systems slowly began to take shape, with more and more funds allocated to building schools for Black children. At long last, there were more local options for Black families, and a larger portion of the Black population was getting access to schools in local neighborhoods, funded by local taxes.

As these external factors were taking shape, something remarkable was happening: by the 1930s, Black segregated schools, many of which had sprouted during Reconstruction, had nurtured generations of graduates. These schools—Lucy Craft Laney's Haines Institute, Mary McLeod Bethune's Daytona Institute, Charlotte Hawkins Brown's Palmer Memorial Institute, to name a few—had done more than simply teach kids how to read and write. They had cultivated great minds, prepared Black students for higher education, and sent them on to HBCUs like Fisk, Spelman, Howard, North Carolina A&T, and Lincoln University. Some graduates even crossed into predominantly white institutions in the North such as Amherst, Vassar, Brown, and Columbia Universities.

Meanwhile, the Harlem Renaissance had introduced a deluge of Black genius into American popular culture. A generation of Black intellectuals, artists, and writers—people like Zora Neale Hurston, Aaron Douglas, and Langston Hughes—took their brilliance to the streets, mainstreaming Black intellectualism and culture. This cultural proliferation fortified the value of Black history and culture as essential to the soul of the nation. By this time, a deep bench of Black educators and leaders had emerged, ready to join the valiant battle for the Black mind.

As new generations came of age, they seized the issues of their day. Black students began to organize and demand more from their universities. They wanted their academic training to expand, for their schools to offer a wider array of courses so that the curricula at HBCUs mirrored the breadth of subjects offered at other historically white colleges. This demand came from within—from Black youth who craved a chance to study fine art, literature, and the sciences. And many schools began to respond to their demands.

Even institutions like Hampton and Tuskegee, which had long been rooted in industrial education, began to shift. By the late 1920s, Hampton added programs in librarianship, business, education, and music. And in 1949—a full eighty years after its founding—the institution appointed its first Black president to usher the school into modern times. Under his leadership, the agricultural trades and industrial programs that had once defined Hampton were phased out, making way for STEM fields like math, chemistry, engineering, and physics to take root.

This shift speaks to a long-standing truth: Black people have always valued education, and they have been willing to fight for it— even when that fight meant challenging one another. Education has been central to the Black freedom struggle, and this era of the battle for the Black mind was no exception. As time went on, support for industrial education waned and new educational issues captured the attention of Black America.

In 1930, during Howard University's graduation ceremony, three gray-haired veterans shared the stage—W. E. B. Du Bois, Lucy Craft Laney, and Robert Russa Moton. They were all there to receive honorary doctorates from the prestigious HBCU, recognizing their lifetime achievements and contributions to Black education. The symbolism of these three sitting together on that stage was powerful. Over the decades, they had clashed, debated, and battled; however, they shared the same fundamental goal of Black liberation through education.

Their pathways had been different, but their commitment was the same. This moment was a testament to their shared vision, and by this point they were no longer warriors, but elders. They had done their part, and fought their fight. Now, it was time for the next generation to carry the torch and continue the fight for Black minds and futures.

Not long after receiving her honorary doctorate from Howard University, Lucy Craft Laney's life came to an end. She passed away in 1933, fifty years after starting her first class in that Augusta church basement. Over the course of five decades, Laney had graduated thousands of Black students from her high school, as well as founded Georgia's first Black nursing school to ensure Black communities would not go without access to health care. While her personal legacy endures, her school could not. Haines Institute closed in 1949 due to financial strain, just a little over a decade after Laney's death. Today, the property where Haines once stood has been transformed into a museum dedicated to Laney's life, and the main street of the "Golden Blocks" has been renamed Laney-Walker Boulevard in honor of her legacy.

Charlotte Hawkins Brown, meanwhile, continued to lead Palmer Memorial Institute well into the 1950s, holding on tightly to the school she had built. However, as her health began to decline, she was forced to step down by the school's board. Struggling with memory loss and other issues, Brown reluctantly transferred the school's leadership to a trusted former teacher at Palmer. But, like Haines, Palmer Memorial Institute struggled to survive after its founder's passing. The school closed its doors just fifteen years after Brown's death.

Despite the struggles of some schools, many liberal arts HBCUs continued to thrive and expand their offerings. Atlanta University, for example, broadened its graduate school programs, adding courses in chemistry, the social sciences, and the natural sciences. It was during this time, in 1934, that W. E. B. Du Bois would resign as editor of the NAACP's *The Crisis* magazine and return to Atlanta University as head of the new sociology department. He remained there for another decade before ultimately immigrating to Ghana, where he spent the final years of his life.

★ ★ ★

The first phase of the battle for the Black mind was essentially a cold war of ideas—ideas about who Black people were, both as citizens and as human beings. The questions and battles over education reflected this deeper conflict, centering on what kind of education Black people needed in order to claim their rightful place in society. For many Black Americans, this battle was about securing an education that would provide equal opportunities. It was about obtaining a curriculum that affirmed Black minds, nurtured Black thinkers, and prepared them to lead their communities and compete in an increasingly modern world. It was about cultivating men and women of character and hope, capable of becoming the future leaders of society.

But not everyone saw it that way. Most whites believed that Black people should be relegated to second-class citizenship. They envisioned a system of education that would teach Black people to stay "in their place"—that would silence them, limit their possibilities, and prevent them from challenging the status quo. These ideas were rooted in the belief that Black people were inherently inferior to white people and that the curricula they received should reflect that.

This was the battlefield of the first era of the Black education struggle. People of all races fell on different sides of this ideological fight, and as we saw, some of them eventually evolved in their thinking. Many came to realize they shared a common goal: that Black Americans gain the freedom to which they were entitled.

The Tuskegee model became less relevant and eventually faded from prominence in the US. However, several of the philanthropists and educators who once invested in Black schools turned their attention to Africa, where the "Negro problem" was seen as a more pressing issue. There, new battles for the Black mind began to emerge.

In South Africa, it wasn't until 1948 when the Apartheid regime took power that Fort Hare University—the country's first HBCU—was stripped of its liberal arts curriculum and replaced with a Bantu education system. This oppressive system resembled an even more vicious form of industrial education, one that drained academic and intellectual life from schools entirely, starting from first grade through university. Apartheid officially began in South Africa right at a time when the civil rights movement in America was gaining momentum. Black people in America were on their way to a new freedom, while our Black brothers and sisters in South Africa hadn't yet hit the lowest point of their racial oppression. Still, our struggles remain connected. Jim Crow and Apartheid—they're cousins, products of the same system of white supremacy.

And what became of Thomas Jesse Jones, the so-called evil genius of the Negro race? He continued his work throughout Africa, gaining international acclaim from European governments. He remained influential through his association with the Phelps-Stokes Fund, publishing several books on his educational philosophies for Black people and Native Americans. But in the end, he died the way he lived: a nobody. Despite his prominence during his lifetime, his name faded into obscurity. Today, his legacy is left without a trace.

Let's keep it that way.

CHAPTER 12

Small Axe

There's a popular Jamaican saying: "Small axe fall big tree." That was the strategy Black communities across America embraced to ensure that the next generation of Black minds would have a real chance at a robust, equal education. It was about demanding that the United States finally live up to its promises of equality, liberty, and justice for *all* citizens. Not just some, and not just those of a certain race. If we were citizens, as the Fourteenth Amendment affirmed, then we needed to be citizens all the way. This new battle was the demand for full equality under the law. Not "soon come," but "right now."

Throughout this book, we've explored what it means to play the long game. We saw how the Tuskegee Machine carefully laid out a strategy, dating to the late 1800s, and how its leaders used that plan to try to control Black education and Black minds worldwide for decades. Well, Black people also know how to play the long game, evident through the long road to *Brown v. Board of Education.*

Most Americans today have heard of *Brown* in school. It's the landmark Supreme Court decision of the twentieth century, the 1954 ruling that overturned *Plessy v. Ferguson* (1896) and declared that any school that is legally separate is necessarily unequal. This decision rang a death knell to Jim Crow, as Supreme Court rulings in one arena have a way of reverberating through every aspect of American life. Although *Brown* was a case focused on public education, the ruling quickly transformed standards across American society: suddenly, separate and unequal was unacceptable in transportation, restaurants, theaters, workplaces, the military, and beyond.

Brown laid the foundation for a cascade of civil rights legislation that finally opened doors that had long been closed to Black Americans. And those doors didn't just open for Black people—they opened for immigrants, women, religious minorities, and other marginalized communities too.

Black American's perseverance, strategy, and bodacious freedom dreams paved the way for a better, more inclusive future for everyone.

At the heart of this battle was Charles Hamilton Houston—the Jim Crow Grim Reaper. He was the architect and mastermind behind the legal strategy that would ultimately lead to *Brown v. Board of Education*. What often gets left out of the history books is that Houston set his plan in motion twenty-five years before that historic decision ever became a reality. He saw the path forward and began laying the groundwork patiently, stone by stone, knowing that dismantling Jim Crow would take more than a quick strike—it would take a movement.

From the beginning, Houston was playing the long game.

He became the dean of Howard University Law School in 1930 and made his mission clear from day one: Howard Law would be a boot camp to train a generation of social engineers—civil rights lawyers committed to dismantling the doctrine of "separate but equal."

Among his earliest students were young, brilliant Black minds like Thurgood Marshall and Oliver Hill. He trained them and many others to channel their legal imagination and genius directly into civil rights issues, specifically targeting segregation. And it all started in the school. Case in point, Black education has always been the cornerstone of the Black freedom struggle.

Houston spent five transformative years at Howard before he took his vision to the NAACP, where he became the organization's first general counsel. This was at a pivotal time when the NAACP shifted its focus from combating racial violence to fighting for educational equality. Houston homed in on developing a long-term legal strategy to challenge school segregation, setting his sights on directly attacking *Plessy v. Ferguson*. He immediately recruited some of his former students from Howard, including Hill and Marshall, to join him. Together, they began traveling through the South in the mid-1930s, filming, documenting, and surveying the reality of racial inequality in education on the ground—not just in the Deep South but also in places like Delaware and Washington, DC. They aimed to prove that these inequities weren't limited to the South; they permeated every corner of American life.

As Houston and his team worked, Black communities across the country took notice. They began reaching out to the NAACP's legal team, people like Houston, Marshall, Constance Baker Motley, and Hill, asking them to take up local cases against white boards of education in hopes of creating better educational opportunities for their children. Everyday Black people, inspired by the strategy and empowered with knowledge, were activating themselves, stepping up to wrest their freedom from a system that had denied it for too long. This was no longer just a legal team working through a national organization; it was a legion of small axes coming for a forest of big trees.

Houston captured his strategy for taking down Jim Crow in a powerful metaphor: "Big trees in the legal forest" such as the *Plessy v. Ferguson* decision, "fell only when their roots became so weakened that they could no longer sustain the weight." The NAACP, under Houston's leadership, developed a strategic, step-by-step plan to erode the foundations of segregation law, eventually leading to *Brown v. Board of Education.* But make no mistake: *Brown* was the culmination of decades of coordinated, painstaking work. It wasn't a lightning bolt that struck overnight; it was a carefully executed strategy involving countless Black communities and individuals who believed that freedom was a collective responsibility.

The NAACP adopted a two-pronged strategy. First, the team used *Plessy v. Ferguson* against itself by pushing for "equalization." *Plessy* had justified segregation if facilities were "equal." But everyone knew that Black schools and public institutions were anything but. Through meticulous documentation, the NAACP brought forth cases that exposed the grotesque inequities: Black schools were severely underfunded, the facilities were crumbling, and teachers were often paid a fraction of what their white counterparts received. By demanding that segregated Black schools be made "equal," Houston and his team set out to force these states to confront the true cost of their hypocrisy. They knew the system would collapse under the financial weight of creating truly "separate but equal" facilities across the board.

The second prong was a direct challenge to *Plessy v. Ferguson* itself, arguing that segregation, by its very nature, violated the Fourteenth Amendment's Equal Protection Clause. Through cases argued starting in the mid-1930s they attacked this cornerstone of segregation, bit by bit. Together, these two approaches worked in tandem to create a pressure cooker of contradictions within Jim Crow's legal structure. It wasn't about asking for more segregation; it was about pushing white supremacy to the brink of its own collapse, exposing its hypocrisy and demanding accountability.

One of the pivotal cases was *Briggs v. Elliott* in South Carolina. Houston and his team broke new ground by arguing that segregation wasn't just about physical separation but that it inflicted psychological harm on Black children. Early in this book, we talked about how the social sciences were integral to the battle for the Black mind—and in this case, social science fought on the side of liberation.

Drs. Kenneth and Mamie Clark, two brilliant Black psychologists, used their scholarship to expose the deep psychological wounds segregation inflicted on Black children. They created the now-famous "Doll Test," where Black children were shown a Black doll and a white doll and asked to identify each. The kids had no problem with the basics—"Which one is the Black doll? Which one is the white doll?" They knew the answer. But when the Clarks asked, "Which doll is the good doll?" a troubling pattern emerged. Overwhelmingly, Black children pointed to the white doll as "good" and the Black doll as "bad."[1] This painful self-identification study was run hundreds of times with Black children across the country, producing the same heartbreaking result again and again.

What Kenneth and Mamie Clark showed the world was that segregation didn't just deny Black children access to resources; it poisoned their self-image. And evidence like this became a powerful tool in court. In *Briggs v. Elliott*, the white judge took a groundbreaking stance, stating that the disparities created by "separate but equal" was a constitutional violation. For the first time on record, a judge declared that segregation was inherently unequal, saying, segregation itself is "per se inequality."[2] Nonetheless, he was in no position to reverse a federal law. Victory would have to wait.

But this kind of truth telling came at a price. The Black families who dared to participate in these cases sacrificed almost everything. The Briggs family, for instance—both husband and wife—lost their jobs simply for having the audacity to stand up for their children's rights. They were driven out of town, their home burned to the ground. This wasn't unique to them; countless other Black families faced harassment, violence, and exile for stepping forward. And still, they persisted.

But this fight wasn't confined to the Deep South. Other cases came out of places like Washington, DC, and Delaware—*"small axe fall big trees."*

Through the 1930s, 1940s, and into the early 1950s, the NAACP's legal strategy, driven by fearless Black lawyers like Constance Baker Motley and Thurgood Marshall, continued with unrelenting courage. And as the years passed, Jim Crow's roots began to rot.

One case that often gets overlooked in this history is the story of the powerful protest ignited by more than four hundred Black students at Robert Russa Moton High School in Farmville, Virginia—a movement led by a courageous high school senior named Barbara Johns. What these students accomplished was groundbreaking, as it is arguably the first true legal victory on the path to *Brown*.[3]

Robert Russa Moton High School was a segregated Black high school in Prince Edward County, Virginia. The building was designed to hold 150 students, but by 1951, it was bursting at the seams with 456 students crammed into its inadequate space. The conditions were horrific. In winter, classrooms were freezing, and in spring, they were unbearably hot. The building leaked, and there was no indoor plumbing, no running water, and no indoor toilets. Parents had been pleading with the local school board for years to fund a new Black high school, but the all-white board ignored their calls.

But they were going to hear Barbara Johns. As a sixteen-year-old high school senior, she organized a small group of her classmates into a committee to strategize a protest. They conspired in secret to plan, waiting until teachers had left the grounds, then holding meetings with the whole student body. They organized a strike, where students left the school and marched downtown to city hall, holding picket signs and demanding a new school building where they could actually learn. This protest didn't immediately yield results, but it galvanized the community, energizing the students and encouraging their parents to stand firm.

Eventually, Barbara Johns and her classmates reached out to the NAACP, hoping it would take their case. After some discussion, Oliver Hill and other NAACP lawyers made them a proposition: the NAACP was no longer fighting for segregated Black schools. It was targeting segregation itself. If Barbara and her classmates were willing to fight for desegregation rather than for only a new Black school, the NAACP would stand with them. After much discussion and careful deliberation, many of the students and their parents agreed.

The NAACP knew it wouldn't win this case, especially in a segregated community with an all-white school board, judge, and jury. But winning wasn't the immediate goal. This was about setting a precedent and creating a public record—each case another small axe chipping away at the dense forest of racial segregation.

Yet, once again, the cost was steep. For many Black families who participated, this fight altered the entire trajectory of their lives. Barbara Johns, for instance, was forced to flee her hometown. She and her family faced death threats, and the Ku Klux Klan showed up at Robert Russa Moton High, burning crosses on the lawn.

But their case planted a seed that grew into a movement, feeding directly into dozens of other cases that dealt Jim Crow its final blow. When *Brown* reached the Supreme Court, it culminated in a unanimous decision that declared, once and for all, that separate is inherently unequal and mandated the desegregation of public schools across the United States.

However, this victory was met with fierce resistance. White Americans across the country vowed that their children would never go to school with Black kids. Local politicians called the ruling tyranny, openly refusing to obey the new law. And in the final decision, a curious clause appeared: desegregation was to be implemented "with all deliberate speed." This phrase allowed white communities to determine their own timelines, and for many, that meant resisting desegregation for as long as possible.[4]

Brown may have ended segregation on paper, but the battle for educational access was far from over.

When left in the hands of openly racist and segregationist white school boards, the enforcement of *Brown v. Board of Education* on the ground was predictably delayed or outright denied. White violence, protest, and defiance erupted across the country. We've all seen those haunting images of Black children simply trying to go to school: Six-year-old Ruby Bridges became the first Black child to integrate a school in Louisiana. To do so she had to be escorted by National Guard soldiers to protect her from the screaming white mobs who were outraged by her very existence. And yet, she did it—not only for herself but for all of us. Then, there was the Little Rock Nine in Arkansas in 1957, those brave Black students who walked through the gauntlet of hateful white classmates and parents to open the doors for future generations. Vivian Malone and James Hood were the first Black students to integrate the University of Alabama, again under protection of the attorney general and a full motorcade of federal marshals. They, too, faced relentless hostility and threats. But they did it anyway. And while these moments were often accompanied by violence, not every form of resistance looked like a mob or a riot.

Even in cases where violence wasn't a factor, Black families sacrificed deeply to force this country to live up to its ideals.

And who were the foot soldiers that had to dismantle the walls of Jim Crow in America's schools? Black children.

The adults—the parents, the lawyers, the community leaders—waged this battle in courtrooms and in NAACP board meetings, but it was Black children who walked into those hostile classrooms. I want you to sit with that for a moment. Imagine if that were your child walking into a school where their teachers, classmates, and parents of their peers didn't want them there. Imagine them facing that with no comfort from familiar Black teachers, no support from family members to accompany them through those doors. That was the burden that Black *children of integration* bore alone.

This story is personal for me because my parents went through it. Both my mother and father, Richard Brown and Arnita Davis Brown, along with all my aunts and uncles, attended the "Lynch Colored School" in Kentucky. They grew up in a segregated school system, and when they speak about it, I can hear the pride and value they placed in their Black school. It was a sanctuary. All their teachers were Black. They lived in their community and were more than just educators—they were neighbors, church members, and role models. They instilled high expectations, discipline, and a deep sense of care in their students. That nurturing environment was sacrificed on the altar of school desegregation.

For my father, that sacrifice became painfully real in ninth grade when the announcement came down that Lynch Colored School would close its doors forever. Principal John Coleman declared that the last class would graduate that year, and my father, along with his classmates, would be sent to the white school. Their school, which had been the heart of their community, was abruptly closed. My parents' school didn't desegregate until 1963—nearly ten years after *Brown* mandated it. That's how deep the resistance to integration ran, and what "all deliberate speed" looked like on the ground.

When my parents' generation was sent up to the white schools, their teachers couldn't go with them. Most Black teachers, with only a handful of exceptions, lost their jobs. The schools didn't need or want to replicate that staff, and so these students walked into a world that was entirely new, entirely white—from the teachers to most of their classmates. And for the most part, they didn't want them there. Black children weren't given the same care nor were they extended the same benefit of the doubt in classrooms. Some teachers went as far as to ignore Black students, refusing to even acknowledge them when they raised their hands as though they were invisible.

They'd left behind a world where teachers knew their families, where there was a shared community, and where cultural understanding ran deep. Their new teachers and classmates didn't live in the same neighborhoods, didn't attend the same churches, and certainly didn't see the students as children for whom they were responsible. For that first generation of integration, the price of the ticket was high.

To this day, for some, just thinking about what they went through brings tears. They mourn not only the personal hardships but also the loss of their own Black schools. The intimacy and cultural strength those schools provided was something precious. But as they reflect, they understand that with integration, Black Americans both lost and gained. We lost many of our own cultural institutions, and with them, some Black businesses and communities also suffered.[5]

We were no longer bound by the legal ties of segregation. In a post-*Brown* society, we had to find new ways to build solidarity—grounded in love, shared struggle, and choice. Yet some would argue that under these new circumstances, Black identity and culture lost some of its strength and cohesiveness. Integration undeniably changed what it meant to be Black in America.

★ ★ ★

The struggle over the Black mind has been a defining feature of each generation's fight. After my parents' generation, it was Black students in the 1960s and 1970s who took up a different kind of fight. They weren't just trying to enter white schools—they were trying to make sure that those schools represented them too. With larger Black and brown student populations finally making it into K–12 schools and onto historically white university campuses, these students organized and protested to demand inclusive education, demanding curricula that reflected the histories, contributions, and cultures of Black people.[6]

This fight culminated in the establishment of Black Studies departments across colleges and universities by the late 1960s. These programs became intellectual engines within many school systems, valuing and reflecting Black contributions in the US and across the diaspora. Today, as a professor, I see that legacy in my own students— decades later, the movement lives on.

My students today are fighting a different battle, one that centers on decolonizing the curriculum and transforming education from the roots up. They are intent on examining the historical foundations of colonization, slavery, and racial capitalism, revealing how those legacies persist and loom large over us today. This generation is focused on dismantling systems of ideological oppression, calling for a curriculum that reflects not just Black American experiences but broad global perspectives. They challenge why our campus buildings bear the names of long-dead white men, figures who often represent histories of exclusion and oppression, rather than the people—our ancestors, including those who were enslaved—upon whose blood and bodies these institutions were built.

They're asking questions that demand justice and recognition: What were the contributions of our ancestors? What does true repair look like in this moment? They are pushing for access, representation, and a profound sense of belonging. And they're not waiting around—they're demanding change now.

With this generation of young Black minds, I am confident, as the great Dr. Jessica B. Harris once said: "The relay is assured."

Epilogue

Where Do We Go from Here?

Thank you so much for riding with me through this epic journey of the battle for the Black mind. This story is essential for all of us—not just to know our history but to realize that we are still in it.

As of this writing, we're in a second Donald Trump era, and this time, it's not just about him. He's backed by a vast, well-organized right-wing conservative movement with a playbook in hand to reshape America's future. Through initiatives like Project 2025, they've drawn up a chilling vision, and education is at the center of it. This isn't just some vague proposal—it's a specific blueprint that includes dismantling the Department of Education, slashing funding for public schools, and gutting policies that promote diversity, equity, and inclusion. These are protections that our communities fought, sacrificed, and risked their lives for.

And it doesn't stop there. The "Stop Woke" laws, which started in Florida, are spreading across states like wildfire, introducing legislation to whitewash history, erase systemic racism from school curricula, and prevent teachers from discussing race and gender in any meaningful way. Combined with Project 2025, these laws set the stage for an education system that actively denies our children the chance to understand their history, their struggles, and their contributions.

Then there's the terrifying surge in book bans sweeping through our public schools and libraries. Black literature, especially, has been a prime target—imagine a world where it's illegal for your child to encounter the transformative words of Toni Morrison, Nikki Giovanni, James Baldwin, Maya Angelou, or even contemporary authors like George M. Johnson. These bans aim to close off worlds, silence voices, and erase our narratives from the shelves. They're not just banning books—they're banning brilliant Black minds.

But I don't want you to leave this book feeling defeated. Together, these efforts should send a chill down your spine, and they should also put you into action mode. Remember that our ancestors gave us everything we need—our own strategies, our own playbook, and our own wisdom to face any threats that come our way.

We've seen movements like this before, and we know what to do. The path may look different, the cast of characters may have changed, and the systems may be more complex, but the core of our fight remains the same.

I've pulled together ten lessons from the chapters in this book as a practical guide we can all carry forward.

We are currently in a new phase in the battle for the Black mind. Our ancestors showed us how to persevere, and now it's our responsibility to continue on—not just to survive in this moment but to thrive. We are our ancestor's wildest dreams.

Where Do We Go from Here?
10 Lessons from Our Ancestors
#1: Get Organized

Throughout the battle for the Black mind, we've seen the power that comes from being organized. Black people have always found strength in forming Black-led organizations and institutions, like the Niagara Movement, fraternities and sororities that make up the Divine Nine, and the NAACP. These organizations served as spaces to strategize, set agendas, and build collective power. Whether in all-Black spaces or multiracial alliances, organizing has always been a source of our strength. That's where we set our strategy, make our demands, and build the foundation for change.

#2: Get in Community

Being in community is a cornerstone of Black culture, and it's something we need to cherish and protect. Community means more than just being in groups—it's about holding a sense of collective responsibility to one another. Share resources, share information, share networks, and stay connected. Our Black school founders, like Mary McLeod Bethune and Charlotte Hawkins Brown, understood this deeply. Competing for the same resources, they still leaned on each other for support, encouragement, and wisdom. In sisterhood, they shared strategies and curricula, and they even sent notes of strength to uplift each other. We need that now more than ever.

#3: Demand Equity

We know that gradual approaches to freedom don't work. Power isn't something given away—it's taken when people demand it. We are full citizens of this country and have every right to demand equity and justice. Don't fall for any ideas of accommodation or acceptance based on "acting right" or staying quiet. Equity and justice are ours to demand, and we have earned them over the generations.

#4: Support Black Institutions

Our Black institutions matter. Whether it's a Black church, cultural institution, archives, museum, or school. Organizations like the National Urban League, the Legal Defense Fund, and the NAACP are important for the vision and advocacy they provide. Do your research on these institutions and others, understand the visions they're setting, and lean into that work. Be active and engaged, because they play a crucial role in our communities.

#5: Don't Sleep on Historically Black Colleges and Universities (HBCUs)

HBCUs have produced more Black professionals than any other educational system in this country. They've been engines of upward mobility for Black people here and abroad. And they are cultural treasures. They've educated our doctors, lawyers, librarians, poets, engineers, scientists, and more, and they're also places that preserve our history and heritage. Especially in a post-2023 world where race-conscious college admissions are under attack,

HBCUs have always been institutions that counted us in. They are world-class and premier—don't you count them out.

#6: Play the Long Game

We've seen how the long game has worked for both sides. The Tuskegee Machine put a plan in place to maintain control over Black minds, playing a long game with each person having a role in the larger strategy. Black leaders like Charles Hamilton Houston also played the long game in crafting the legal strategy that led to *Brown v. Board of Education*. It took twenty-five years to bring that vision to life. Project 2025 is a long-term playbook designed to capture and dismantle American democracy. What's our counterstrategy? We need a long game too. Figure out your role—whether it's speaking up, organizing, teaching, or simply holding space. Get in where you fit in, and let's play the long game together.

#7: Play the Short Game

Remember, small axe fall big trees. Think about the actions you can take right now that are within your personal capacity to chip away at the roots of white supremacy. As a Blackademic, my scholarship is my main weapon. I write books, coauthor textbooks, and shape narratives to equip my people with knowledge as a path to freedom. I'm also putting my resources into Black organizations and showing up as a compassionate professor, one who sees the humanity in all my students. So ask yourself: What's within your reach that can help push us all closer to freedom?

#8: All Money Ain't Good Money

We've seen the strings that have historically come attached to white philanthropy in Black education. That dynamic hasn't gone anywhere—it's just evolved. Today, billionaires wield outsized influence, and those of us with urgency and clarity of purpose may be approached by corporations or think tanks looking to co-opt our work. So develop a vetting process for the financial support you accept. Set clear principles and conditions under which you will or won't engage with certain funders. Make sure you're grounded in your values, not someone else's agenda.

#9: Know Your Opponent

It's exhausting but essential to understand the strategies and intentions of those who oppose our liberation. You can't show up to a basketball game in baseball gear—and the same goes for this battle for the Black mind. Whether you're a parent, educator, student, or nonprofit leader, take time to learn about the long-term plans of those pushing for "anti-woke" legislation, book bans, and systemic erasure. Don't put your head in the sand; we need to keep our eyes open and stay woke so we can strategize and organize accordingly.

#10: Freedom Dream!

Every political movement starts with radical imagination. It's essential to dream about the world you want for yourself and your children. Speak those dreams aloud; write them down; envision them. Remember Mary Smith Peake, who taught enslaved Black people to read under that freedom tree, risking everything to act on her vision. Her world didn't yet exist, but she dared to imagine it—and because she dreamed, she acted. Let's hold onto that same spirit. Remember, we are our ancestors' wildest dreams, and it's on us to keep dreaming and building.

Acknowledgments

I've always been a little shy about writing acknowledgments. In some ways, it feels like saying goodbye to my book—releasing it into the world after holding it close for so long. But it's also a moment to reflect on the journey, to honor the people who helped me carry this story from the quiet spaces of my mind to the pages you hold now.

Writing is my life's work. I will continue to tell Black stories, our stories, until I am no more. But this book has been a long time coming. It demanded more of me than I thought I had to vie—and it reminded me that no great endeavor is ever accomplished alone. To everyone who talked with me, prayed for me, or simply cheered me on from afar, please know that I carry your encouragement in my heart. Here, I offer just a few words of thanks.

To Ian Kleinert, my rainmaker and confidant—you listen, you make time, and you never ask me to take my head out of the clouds. You believe in the power of my dreams, and you work tirelessly to make them real. Thank you for showing me what it means to have someone in your corner who is equally invested in your vision and your spirit.

ACKNOWLEDGMENTS

To the incredible team at Legacy Lit, I could not be prouder to be a part of what you are building. Krishan Trotman, your work is nothing short of revolutionary. With every book you publish, you are rewriting the future of this industry and making space for stories that need to be told. Thank you for believing in me and this book from the very beginning. You read and re-read, pushed and prodded, and made sure it lived up to its promise. You have shown me what excellence in publishing looks like. To Amina Iro and Mahito Henderson—your editorial brilliance and care brought this book to life. Thank you for your sharp minds and steady hands. I am forever grateful to be on this journey with you all.

To RJ Miller, can you believe you have two books under your belt? Believe me when I say, we are just getting started.

To the countless students who have graced my classrooms over the years—your questions, insights, and brilliance shaped this work. To my Emory research assistants—Leo Reale, Aja Moore, Doussou Toure, Ulia Ahn, and Alana Dawson—you helped me unearth treasures in the archives and brought this book to life. To the RARER workshop graduate students—Temi Alao, Umaymah Mohammad, and Jadelynn Zhang—you reminded me why we do this work.

To Russell Rickford, for breathing life back into my situation. And to Keecha Harris and Selassie Atadika—you are my sister's keepers.

To Alyasah, you called me a "writer's writer," and I dared to believe you. Thank you for seeing me. Jamaal, for your quiet presence at every step. And to Marcus and Danté: your boundless love is my anchor.

Mom and Dad—Richard Brown and Arnita Davis Brown—you are my first and forever teachers. I will never stop being your baby, no matter how far I go. Thank you for giving me roots and wings, and for teaching me to cherish the stories of where we come from.

To my ancestors, human and solar, who whisper through the pages of this book. I am because we are.

And finally, to my love, Charly Palmer. You insisted that only I could write this book, and you were right. Thank you for your endless patience, for listening when the words felt heavy, for your generosity of spirit, and for letting me roam the world to gather the threads of this story. You are my Love Supreme.

Note on Archives

This book is rooted in eight years of archival research that took me across the world to uncover the stories, documents, and histories that form its foundation. While I chose to let the narrative lead in these pages, the story is deeply grounded in scholarly rigor and the meticulous study of primary sources.

The majority of my research came from the following archives: the Rockefeller Archives (Tarrytown, NY), the Carnegie Corporation archives (Butler Library, Columbia University), the Phelps-Stokes Fund Archives (Schomburg Center for Black History and Culture), Emory University Archives (Rose Library, Emory University), the Charlotte Hawkins Brown Papers (Schlessinger Library, Harvard), the Lucy Craft Laney Museum (Augusta, GA), Hampton University Archives (Hampton, VA), and the W. E. B. Du Bois Papers (online and at the University of Massachusetts, Amherst).

These archives, along with many others, provided the building blocks for this work. I am indebted to the archivists and institutions that preserve and care for these materials, ensuring that the stories of the past remain accessible to those of us seeking to make sense of the present.

Notes

Introduction

1. Lee C. Bollinger and Geoffrey R. Stone, *A Legacy of Discrimination: The Essential Constitutionality of Affirmative Action* (Oxford University Press, 2023).

2. Carter Godwin Woodson, *The Education of the Negro Prior to 1861: A History of the Education of the Colored People of the United States from the Beginning of Slavery to the Civil War* (Association for the Study of Negro Life and History, 1919).

Chapter 1

1. Herbert Aptheker, *Nat Turner's Slave Rebellion: Including the 1831 "Confessions"* (Courier, 2012).

2. Kay Ann Taylor, "Mary S. Peake and Charlotte L. Forten: Black Teachers during the Civil War and Reconstruction," *Journal of Negro Education* (2005): 124–137.

3. W. E. B. Du Bois, "Of the Training of Black Men," *Atlantic*, September 1, 1902, www.theatlantic.com/magazine/archive/1902/09/of-the-training-of-black-men/531192/.

4. James D. Anderson, *The Education of Blacks in the South, 1860–1935* (Chapel Hill: University of North Carolina Press, 1988).

5. From 1868 to 1877, Hampton briefly experimented with admitting Native American students, though the effort was soon abandoned; Armstrong and his faculty concluded that Native Americans required a different type of instruction.

6. Booker T. Washington, *Up from Slavery*, ed. Jarvis R. Givens (New York: W. W. Norton, 2024).

Chapter 2

1. "U.S. Senate: Freedmen's Bureau Acts of 1865 and 1866," accessed November 9, 2024, www.senate.gov/artandhistory/history/common/generic/Freedmens Bureau.htm; Ronald E. Butchart, *Northern Schools, Southern Blacks, and Reconstruction: Freedmen's Education, 1862–1875* (Westport, CT: Greenwood, 1980); William Edward Burghardt Du Bois, *The Freedmen's Bureau* (Atlantic Monthly, 1901).

2. "National Assessment of Adult Literacy (NAAL)" (National Center for Education Statistics), accessed November 9, 2024, https://nces.ed.gov/naal/lit _history.asp.

3. Robert A. Margo, "Race and Schooling in the South: A Review of the Evidence," in *Race and Schooling in the South, 1880–1950: An Economic History* (University of Chicago Press, 1990), 6–32, www.nber.org/books-and-chapters /race-and-schooling-south-1880-1950-economic-history/race-and-schooling -south-review-evidence.

4. Marcus Anthony Hunter, *Black Citymakers: How the Philadelphia Negro Changed Urban America* (New York: Oxford University Press, 2013); William Cohen, *At Freedom's Edge: Black Mobility and the Southern White Quest for Racial Control, 1861–1915* (Louisiana State University Press, 1991); William Edward Burghardt Du Bois, *Black Reconstruction in America: Toward a History of the Part Which Black Folk Played in the Attempt to Reconstruct Democracy in America, 1860– 1880* (Transaction, 2013).

5. C. Vann Woodward, *The Strange Career of Jim Crow* (New York: Oxford University Press, 1955); Du Bois, *Black Reconstruction in America*.

6. Du Bois, *Black Reconstruction in America*.

7. A. DuVernay, S. Averick, and H. Barish, "13th [Documentary]," *US: Net-flix*, 2016; Douglas A. Blackmon, *Slavery by Another Name: The Re-Enslavement of Black Americans from the Civil War to World War II* (Anchor, 2009); W. E. B. Du Bois, "The Spawn of Slavery: The Convict Lease System in the South," *Missionary Review of the World* 14 (1901): 737–745.

8. Steering Committee on Slavery and Justice, "Slavery and Justice: Report of the Brown University Steering Committee on Slavery and Justice" (Brown University, 2007).

Chapter 3

1. Dylan C. Penningroth, *The Claims of Kinfolk: African American Property and Community in the Nineteenth-Century South* (University of North Carolina Press Books, 2004); Karen Cook Bell, "African American Freedom and the Illusive 'Forty Acres and a Mule' - AAIHS," November 16, 2017, www.aaihs.org /african-american-freedom-and-the-illusive-forty-acres-and-a-mule/.

2. "Booker T. Washington Delivers the 1895 Atlanta Compromise Speech," accessed November 10, 2024, https://historymatters.gmu.edu/d/39/.

3. In Malcolm X's 1963 speech "Message to the Grassroots," he described the predicament of some slaves identifying more with their so-called master than with themselves:

> To understand this, you have to go back to what [the] young brother here referred to as the house Negro and the field Negro—back during slavery. There was two kinds of slaves. There was the house Negro and the field Negro. The house Negroes—they lived in the house with master, they dressed pretty good, they ate good 'cause they ate his food—what he left. They lived in the attic or the basement, but still they lived near the master; and they loved their master more than the master loved himself. They would give their life to save the master's house quicker than the master would. The house Negro, if the master said, "We got a good house here," the house Negro would say, "Yeah, we got a good house here." Whenever the master said "we," he said "we." That's how you can tell a house Negro. If the master's house caught on fire, the house Negro would fight harder to put the blaze out than the master would. If the master got sick, the house Negro would say, "What's the matter, boss, we sick?" We sick! He identified himself with his master more than his master identified with himself.

4. William Edward Burghardt Du Bois, *The Philadelphia Negro: A Social Study*, 14 (University of Pennsylvania Press, 1899).

5. Booker T. Washington, ed., *The Negro Problem* (New York: Firework, 2015).

6. Pero Gaglo Dagbovie, "Exploring a Century of Historical Scholarship on Booker T. Washington," *Journal of African American History* 92, no. 2 (2007): 239–264.

7. Kerri Greenidge, "The Radical Black Newspaper That Declared 'None Are Free Unless All Are Free,'" *Guardian*, January 3, 2020, US News, www.theguardian .com/us-news/2020/jan/03/boston-guardian-william-monroe-trotter-newspaper.

8. W. E. B. Du Bois, *The Souls of Black Folk* (Chicago: A. C. McClurg, 1903).

9. White readers were often complimentary of the overall message of the book but quick to police Du Bois's tone. For instance, one review in the *American Annals of Political and Social Science* praised the book but criticized Du Bois for his "mental bitterness" and the straightforward manner in which he wrote about racism and white supremacy. The reviewer suggested that Du Bois's sharpness, particularly in his criticism of Washington, was a liability, saying that Du Bois would only gain real influence when he stopped carrying a "chip on his shoulder." This kind of criticism from white scholars—essentially telling a Black intellectual to tone down their righteous anger about racism—was all too common. And while the review acknowledged that Washington's educational program might be narrow, it still placed the burden of overcoming racial prejudice on Black people alone. According to the reviewer, "Race prejudice . . . will cease when the Blacks can command and compel the respect and sympathy of the whites."

10. Kerri K. Greenidge, *Black Radical: The Life and Times of William Monroe Trotter* (New York: Liveright, 2019).

11. W. E. B. Du Bois, "Letter from W. E. B. Du Bois to George Foster Peabody," December 28, 1903, MS 312, Special Collections and University Archives, University of Massachusetts Amherst Libraries.

12. W. E. B. Du Bois, "Letter from W. E. B. Du Bois to Joanna P. Moore," April 2, 1907, MS 312, Special Collections and University Archives, University of Massachusetts Amherst Libraries.

13. Booker T. Washington, "Tuskegee Student Letter of Complaint to Booker T. Washington" (Manuscript Division, Library of Congress, Washington, D.C. Library of Congress, 1904), Booker T. Washington papers, 1853–1946; Box 905 Reel 683, Library of Congress.

14. Arthur F. Raper, *The Tragedy of Lynching* (New York: Dover, 1933); Ida B. Wells, *Southern Horrors: Lynch Law in All Its Phases* (Floating, 2014).

Chapter 4

1. Audrey Thomas McCluskey, "'We Specialize in the Wholly Impossible': Black Women School Founders and Their Mission," *Signs: Journal of Women in Culture and Society* 22, no. 2 (1997): 403–426; Audrey Thomas McCluskey, *A Forgotten Sisterhood: Pioneering Black Women Educators and Activists in the Jim Crow South* (Lanham, MD: Rowman & Littlefield, 2014).

2. Sean Joiner and Gerald Smith, *Augusta* (Mount Pleasant, SC: Arcadia, 2012).

3. "The Lucy Craft Laney Museum of Black History | Golden Blocks," accessed November 10, 2024, https://lucycraftlaneymuseum.com/golden-blocks/.

4. *Cummings v. Richmond County Board of Education*, No. 164 (Supreme Court of United States, December 18, 1899).

5. Lucy Craft Laney, "Letter from Lucy C. Laney to W. E. B. Du Bois," March 26, 1911, MS 312, Special Collections and University Archives, University of Massachusetts Amherst Libraries.

6. W. E. B. Du Bois, *Dusk of Dawn: An Essay toward an Autobiography of a Race Concept: The Oxford WEB Du Bois* (New Brunswick: Transaction, 1940).

7. "Miss Lucy Laney Is Unique Leader of Race: Has Established Most Outstanding Secondary School in Country for Colored Youth," *Afro-American (1893–)*, June 12, 1926.

Chapter 5

1. Jarvis R. Givens, *Fugitive Pedagogy: Carter G. Woodson and the Art of Black Teaching* (Harvard University Press, 2021); "ABOUT COLORED TEACHERS ASSOCIATIONS," Black Teacher Archive—CURIOSity Digital Collections, July 17, 2023, https://curiosity.lib.harvard.edu/black-teacher-archive/feature/about-colored-teachers-associations.

2. Vanessa Siddle Walker, *Hello Professor: A Black Principal and Professional Leadership in the Segregated South* (University of North Carolina Press, 2009); Karida L. Brown, *Gone Home: Race and Roots through Appalachia* (Chapel Hill, NC: University of North Carolina Press, 2018).

3. Nannie Helen Burroughs, *Nannie Helen Burroughs: A Documentary Portrait of an Early Civil Rights Pioneer, 1900–1959* (University of Notre Dame Press, 2019); Leigh Soares, "Margaret Murray Washington: The Life and Times of a

Career Clubwoman by Sheena Harris," *Journal of Southern History* 88, no. 2 (2022): 403–404.

4. Beverly W. Jones, "Mary Church Terrell and the National Association of Colored Women, 1896 to 1901," *Journal of Negro History* 67, no. 1 (April 1982): 20–33, https://doi.org/10.2307/2717758; Alison M. Parker, *Unceasing Militant: The Life of Mary Church Terrell* (University of North Carolina Press Books, 2020).

5. Audrey Thomas McCluskey, "Mary McLeod Bethune and the Education of Black Girls," *Sex Roles* 21, nos. 1–2 (1989): 113–126; Mary McLeod Bethune, *Mary McLeod Bethune: Building a Better World, Essays and Selected Documents* (Indiana University Press, 2001).

6. McCluskey, "Bethune and the Education of Black Girls"; Audrey Thomas McCluskey, *A Forgotten Sisterhood: Pioneering Black Women Educators and Activists in the Jim Crow South* (Lanham, MD: Rowman & Littlefield, 2014).

7. McCluskey, *Forgotten Sisterhood.*

8. Charlotte Hawkins Brown Museum, "A Day in the Life of a Palmerite," *Medium* (blog), February 23, 2022, https://chbmuseum.medium.com/a-day-in -the-life-of-a-palmerite-6ce1526a57e1.

9. Charles Weldon Wadelington and Richard F. Knapp, *Charlotte Hawkins Brown & Palmer Memorial Institute: What One Young African American Woman Could Do* (University of North Carolina Press Books, 1999); McCluskey, *Forgotten Sisterhood.*

10. *2020 Virtual Palmer Memorial Institute Alumni Reunion*, 2020, www.you tube.com/watch?v=dwuapU6g9m8.

11. Wadelington and Knapp, *Charlotte Hawkins Brown & Palmer Memorial Institute.*

12. Henry Louis Gates and Gene Andrew Jarrett, *The New Negro: Readings on Race, Representation, and African American Culture, 1892–1938* (Princeton, NJ: Princeton University Press, 2007).

Chapter 6

1. Mark S. Granovetter, "The Strength of Weak Ties," *American Journal of Sociology* 78, no. 6 (May 1973): 1360–1380, https://doi.org/10.1086/225469.

2. Langston Hughes, *I Wonder as I Wander: An Autobiographical Journey* (Macmillan, 1993); Noliwe M. Rooks, *A Passionate Mind in Relentless Pursuit: The Vision of Mary McLeod Bethune* (New York: Penguin Random House, 2024).

3. Audrey Thomas McCluskey, "'We Specialize in the Wholly Impossible': Black Women School Founders and Their Mission," *Signs: Journal of Women in Culture and Society* 22, no. 2 (1997); Darlene Clark Hine, Wilma King, and Linda Reed, *We Specialize in the Wholly Impossible: A Reader in Black Women's History*, vol. 17 (New York University Press, 1995).

4. Charles Weldon Wadelington and Richard F. Knapp, *Charlotte Hawkins Brown & Palmer Memorial Institute: What One Young African American Woman Could Do* (University of North Carolina Press Books, 1999).

Chapter 7

1. Donald Fisher, "The Role of Philanthropic Foundations in the Reproduction and Production of Hegemony: Rockefeller Foundations and the Social Sciences," *Sociology* 17, no. 2 (1983): 206–233.

2. James D. Anderson, "Northern Foundations and the Shaping of Southern Black Rural Education, 1902–1935," *History of Education Quarterly* 18, no. 4 (1978): 371–396; James D. Anderson, *The Education of Blacks in the South, 1860–1935* (Chapel Hill: University of North Carolina Press, 1988); Henry Allen Bullock, *History of Negro Education in the South* (Cambridge, MA: Harvard University Press, 1967).

3. Bullock, *History of Negro Education*; William Henry Watkins, *The White Architects of Black Education: Ideology and Power in America, 1865–1954* (New York: Teachers College Press, 2001).

4. "Black Education and Rockefeller Philanthropy from the Jim Crow South to the Civil Rights Era," *REsource* (blog), accessed November 11, 2024, https://resource.rockarch.org/story/black-education-and-rockefeller-philanthropy-from-the-jim-crow-south-to-the-civil-rights-era/.

5. "$600,000 FOR TUSKEGEE AND B.T. WASHINGTON; Andrew Carnegie's Contribution to the Endowment Fund. Also to Provide Life Income for Mr. and Mrs. Washington—Philanthropist Has Been Giving $10,000 a Year to the Institute.," *New York Times*, April 24, 1903, Archives, www.nytimes.com/1903/04/24/archives/600000-for-tuskegee-and-bt-washington-andrew-carnegies-contribution.html.

6. Andrew Zimmerman, *Alabama in Africa: Booker T. Washington, the German Empire, and the Globalization of the New South* (Princeton, NJ: Princeton University Press, 2010).

7. Robert Trent Vinson, *The Americans Are Coming!: Dreams of African American Liberation in Segregationist South Africa* (Ohio University Press, 2012); Robert Trent Vinson, "'SEA KAFFIRS': 'AMERICAN NEGROES'AND THE GOSPEL OF GARVEYISM IN EARLY TWENTIETH-CENTURY CAPE TOWN," *Journal of African History* 47, no. 2 (2006): 281–303.

8. W. Manning Marable, "Booker T. Washington and African Nationalism," *Phylon (1960–)* 35, no. 4 (1974): 398–406; Manning Marable, "SOUTH AFRICAN NATIONALISM IN BROOKLYN: JOHN L. DUBE'S ACTIVITIES IN NEW YORK STATE, 1887–1899," *Afro-Americans in New York Life and History (1977–1989)* 3, no. 1 (1979): 23; W. Manning Marable, "A Black School in South Africa," *Negro History Bulletin* 37, no. 4 (1974): 258.

9. Andrew Carnegie, *The Negro in America: An Address Delivered before the Philosophical Institution of Edinburgh, 16th October, 1907* (Committee of Twelve for the Advancement of the Interests of the Negro Race, 1907).

10. "New World Bank Report Assesses Sources of Inequality in Five Countries in Southern Africa," Text/HTML, World Bank, accessed November 11, 2024, www.worldbank.org/en/news/press-release/2022/03/09/new-world-bank -report-assesses-sources-of-inequality-in-five-countries-in-southern-africa.

11. Cecil J. Rhodes, *The Last Will and Testament of Cecil John Rhodes: With Elucidatory Notes to Which Are Added Some Chapters Describing the Political and Religious Ideas of the Testator* ("Review of Reviews" Office, 1902).

12. Jeffrey C. Stewart, *The New Negro: The Life of Alain Locke* (New York: Oxford University Press, 2018).

13. Rhodes, *Last Will and Testament.*

Chapter 8

1. William Edward Burghardt Du Bois, *The Philadelphia Negro: A Social Study*, 14 (University of Pennsylvania Press, 1899).

2. Anna Julia Cooper, *The Voice of Anna Julia Cooper: Including a Voice from the South and Other Important Essays, Papers, and Letters* (Rowman & Littlefield, 1998); Carl A. Grant, Keffrelyn D. Brown, and Anthony L. Brown, *Black Intellectual Thought in Education: The Missing Traditions of Anna Julia Cooper, Carter G. Woodson, and Alain Leroy Locke* (New York: Routledge, 2015).

3. Franklin Frazier, *Black Bourgeoisie* (New York: Simon and Schuster, 1997).

4. José Itzigsohn and Karida L. Brown, *The Sociology of W. E. B. Du Bois: Racialized Modernity and the Global Color Line* (New York: New York University Press, 2020).

5. W. E. B. Du Bois, "Thomas Jesse Jones," *The Crisis*, 1921.

6. Franklin H. Giddings, *The Elements of Sociology: A Textbook for Colleges and Schools* (Macmillan, 1898).

7. Franklin H. Giddings, *The Principles of Sociology: An Analysis of the Phenomena of Association and of Social Organization* (Macmillan, 1896).

8. Thomas Jesse Jones, *The Sociology of a New York City Block* (New York: Columbia University Press, 1904).

9. Jones, *Sociology*.

10. Claude S. Fischer, *Inequality by Design: Cracking the Bell Curve Myth* (Princeton University Press, 1996); Lisa Delpit, *Other People's Children: Cultural Conflict in the Classroom* (New Press, 2006); Monika Williams Shealey and Martha Scott Lue, "Why Are All the Black Kids Still in Special Education? Revisiting the Issue of Disproportionate Representation," *Multicultural Perspectives* 8, no. 2 (July 2006): 3–9, https://doi.org/10.1207/s15327892mcp0802_2.

Chapter 9

1. National Park Service, "The Death of Booker T. Washington," n.d., www.nps.gov/bowa/learn/historyculture/upload/the-final-btwdeath-site-bulletin.pdf.

2. Pero Gaglo Dagbovie, "Exploring a Century of Historical Scholarship on Booker T. Washington," *Journal of African American History* 92, no. 2 (2007); Louis R. Harlan, *Booker T. Washington: The Wizard of Tuskegee, 1901–1915* (New York: Oxford University Press, 1983); William Fitzhugh Brundage, *Booker T. Washington and Black Progress: Up from Slavery 100 Years Later* (University Press of Florida, 2004); Raymond Smock, *Booker T. Washington in Perspective: Essays of Louis R. Harlan* (University Press of Mississippi, 2006).

3. General Education Board, "Negro Education, Minutes of the Conference of the General Education Board" (General Education Board, November 29, 1915), General Education Board records; FA058, Box 14, Rockefeller Archives, https://

dimes.rockarch.org/xtf/view?docId=ead/FA058/FA058.xml;chunk.id=222b82e
f156340fd8eecf8809693bf6a;doc.view=contents;#35d3ebaf295d4ef9b30da052510
f86b9.

4. James D. Anderson, *The Education of Blacks in the South, 1860–1935* (Chapel
Hill: University of North Carolina Press, 1988).

5. W. E. B. Du Bois, "The Amenia Conference, 1925" (1925), MS 312, Special Collections and University Archives, University of Massachusetts Amherst
Libraries.

Chapter 10

1. Thomas Jesse Jones, *Negro Education: A Study of the Private and Higher
Schools for Colored People in the United States*, vol. 1, 2 vols. (Washington, DC: U.S.
Bureau of Education, 1917).

2. Carter G. Woodson, "Progress in Negro Status and Race Relations, 1911–
1946 the Thirty-Five Year Report of the Phelps Stokes Fund by Anson Phelps
Stokes, Thomas Jesse Jones, J. D. Rheinallt Jones and L. A. Roy," *Journal of Negro
History* 34, no. 3 (1949): 367–369.

Chapter 11

1. B. Joyce Ross, "Mary McLeod Bethune and the National Youth Administration: A Case Study of Power Relationships in the Black Cabinet of Franklin D. Roosevelt," *Journal of Negro History* 60, no. 1 (January 1975): 1–28, https://
doi.org/10.2307/2716791; Jill Watts, *The Black Cabinet: The Untold Story of African
Americans and Politics during the Age of Roosevelt* (Atlantic Monthly, 2020).

Chapter 12

1. Kenneth B. Clark and Mamie P. Clark, "Emotional Factors in Racial
Identification and Preference in Negro Children," *Journal of Negro Education* 19,
no. 3 (1950): 341–350.

2. *Briggs v. Elliott* (United States District Court E. D. South Carolina,
Charleston Division July 15, 1955).

3. Ronald L. Heinemann, "Moton School Strike and Prince Edward County School Closings," Encyclopedia Virginia, accessed November 11, 2024, https://encyclopediavirginia.org/entries/moton-school-strike-and-prince -edward-county-school-closings/.

4. Charles J. Ogletree, *All Deliberate Speed: Reflections on the First Half Century of* Brown v. Board of Education (W. W. Norton, 2004); Derrick Bell, *Silent Covenants:* Brown v. Board of Education *and the Unfulfilled Hopes for Racial Reform* (Oxford University Press, 2004); Karida L. Brown, *Gone Home: Race and Roots through Appalachia* (Chapel Hill, NC: University of North Carolina Press, 2018).

5. Karida L. Brown, "The 'Hidden Injuries' of School Desegregation: Cultural Trauma and Transforming African American Identities," *American Journal of Cultural Sociology* 4, no. 2 (2016): 196–220; "Opinion | When Desegregation Came to Harlan County, Ky.: An Oral History," *Washington Post*, May 28, 2024, www.washingtonpost.com/opinions/2024/05/28/desegregation-brown-v-board -harlan-county/; Brown, *Gone Home.*

6. Martha Biondi, *The Black Revolution on Campus* (University of California Press, 2012); Peniel E. Joseph, "Dashikis and Democracy: Black Studies, Student Activism, and the Black Power Movement," *Journal of African American History* 88, no. 2 (April 2003): 182–203, https://doi.org/10.2307/3559065; Fabio Rojas, *From Black Power to Black Studies: How a Radical Social Movement Became an Academic Discipline* (Baltimore, MD: Johns Hopkins University Press, 2010); Russell Rickford, *We Are an African People: Independent Education, Black Power, and the Radical Imagination* (Oxford University Press, 2016).

1
Introduction

The national minimum wage has a long history in the United States and has been accepted by public opinion. The necessity for periodic raises in the minimum wage to keep pace with the rise in average wages, however, has led to continuing controversy in Congress on how high to set the rates. A mounting volume of scholarly research by economists also has questioned their net benefits.

The social objective of a legal minimum wage is to improve the welfare of the lowest-wage workers. Yet economic theory indicates that demand for labor involves a negative relation of the amount of labor employed to the price of labor, the average hourly wage. In order for the income of workers as a group to be increased by an imposed wage increase, therefore, the disemployment effects for some workers must be small relative to the increased wage for those still employed. This would hold true for a demand elasticity greater than one in absolute value. (Elasticity is defined as the ratio of the percentage change in labor employed to the percentage change in wage.) This results, of course, in an inequitable distribution of effects among workers; so the group benefit should be regarded as a net social gain only if other means are used to compensate the disemployed who are excluded from the wage gains.

Legislators have long been skeptical about the disemployment effects predicted in economic theory. The basic difficulty in learning from historical experience is that the sizes of wage increases imposed by the minimum wage have been very modest in the midst of larger changes in wages and employment due to a multitude of complex forces. Things merely *seem* to get better after each new raise is legislated. This basic difficulty in isolating the effects of a minimum wage has even led some proponents to deny any disemployment effects at all.

Past Research. Early research efforts by economists to isolate minimum-wage effects were concentrated on the extreme cases of very low wage industries and areas where the costs imposed by the minimum wage

1

12 301